Musings

Where Ideas Develop

80 Pages

8.5x11 in.

2021 Tanya Purcell

IDEAS

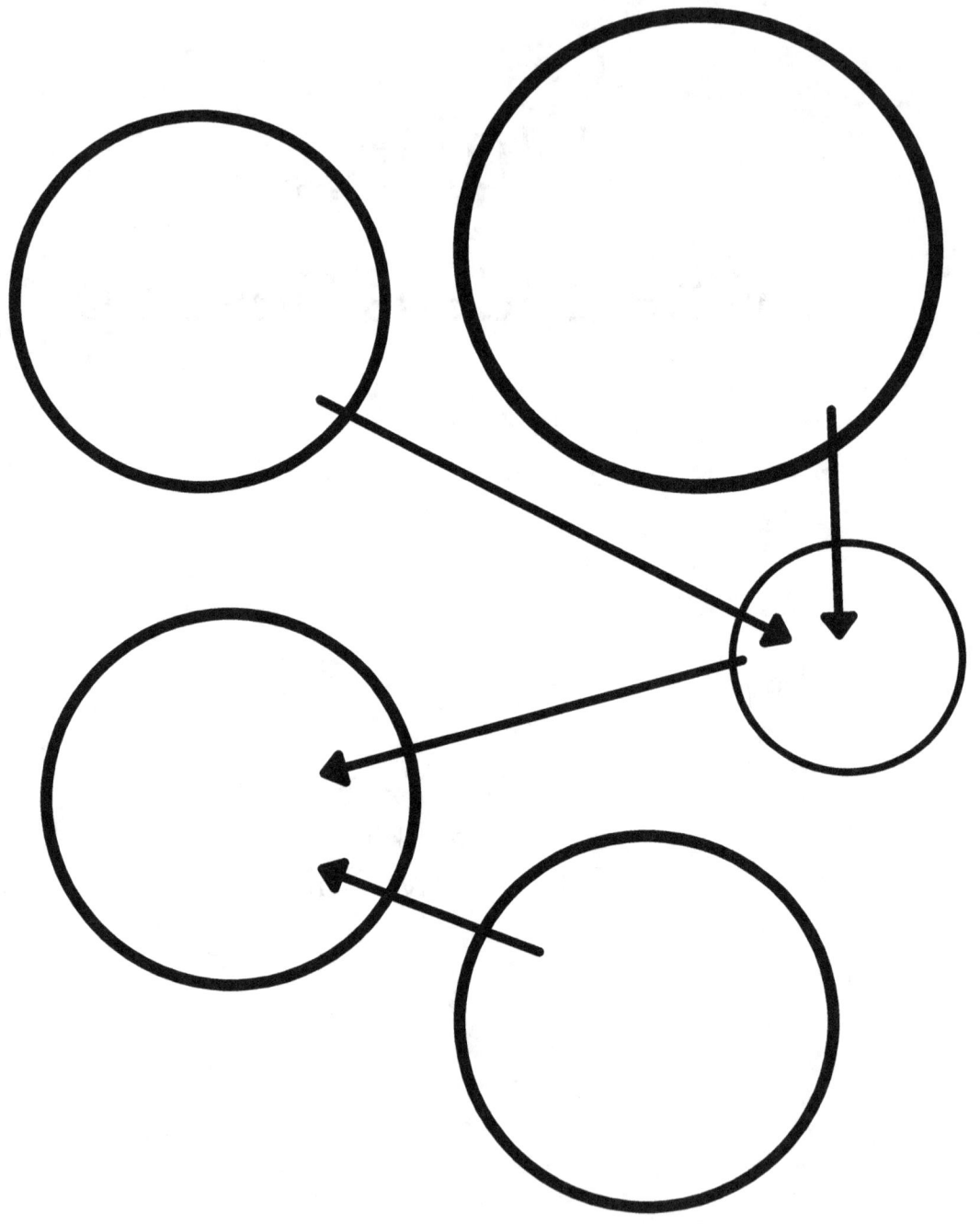

IDEAS

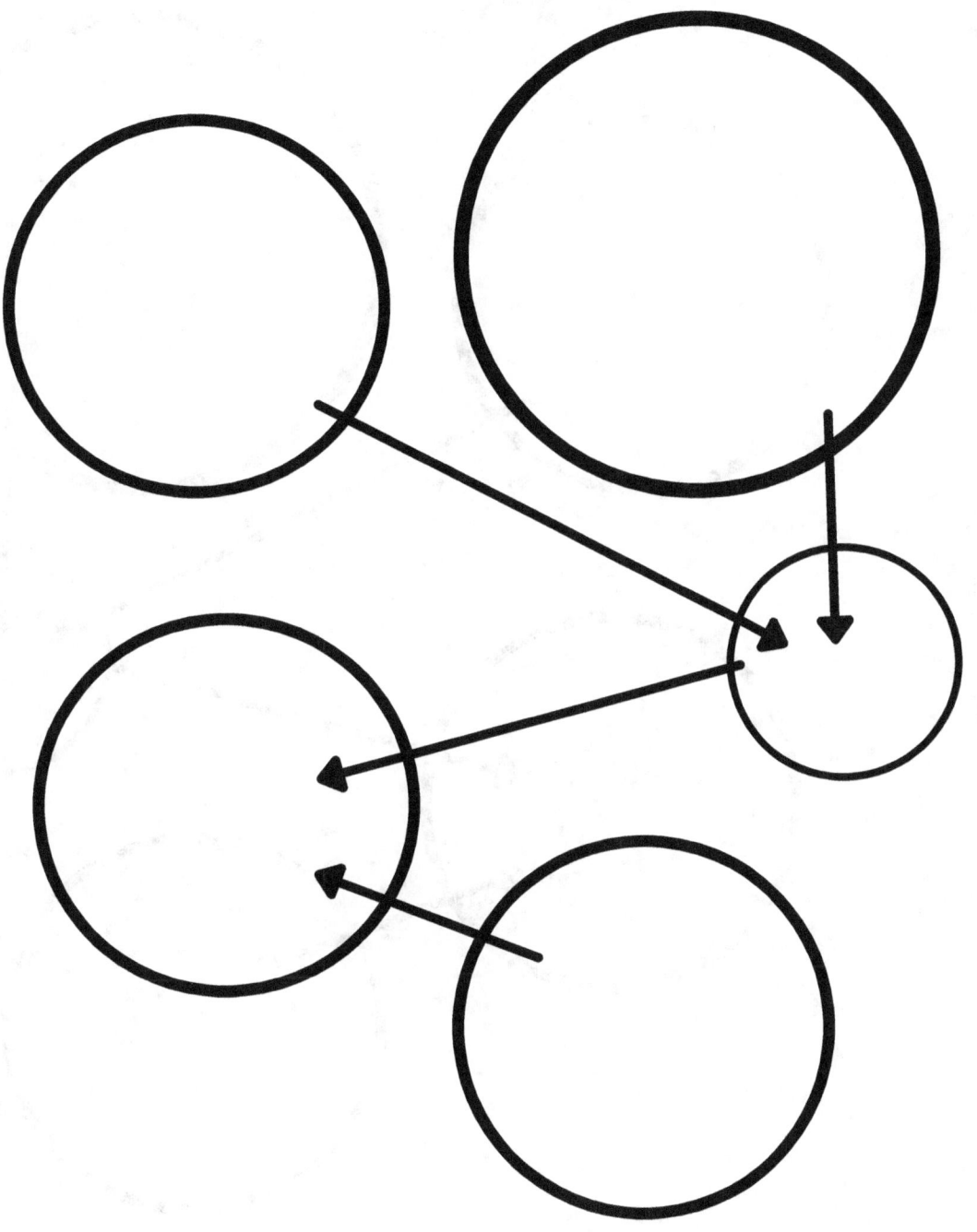

IDEAS

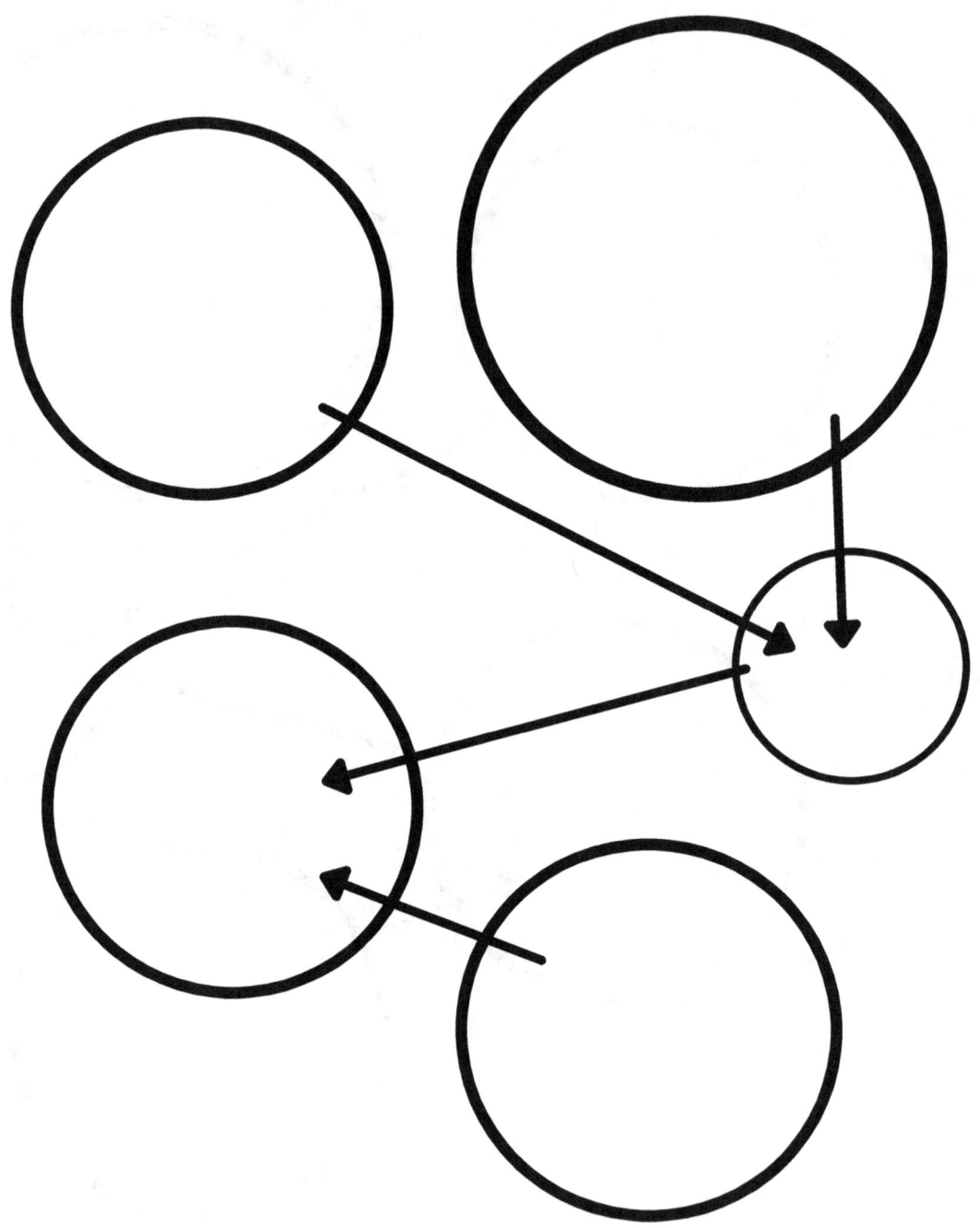

IDEAS

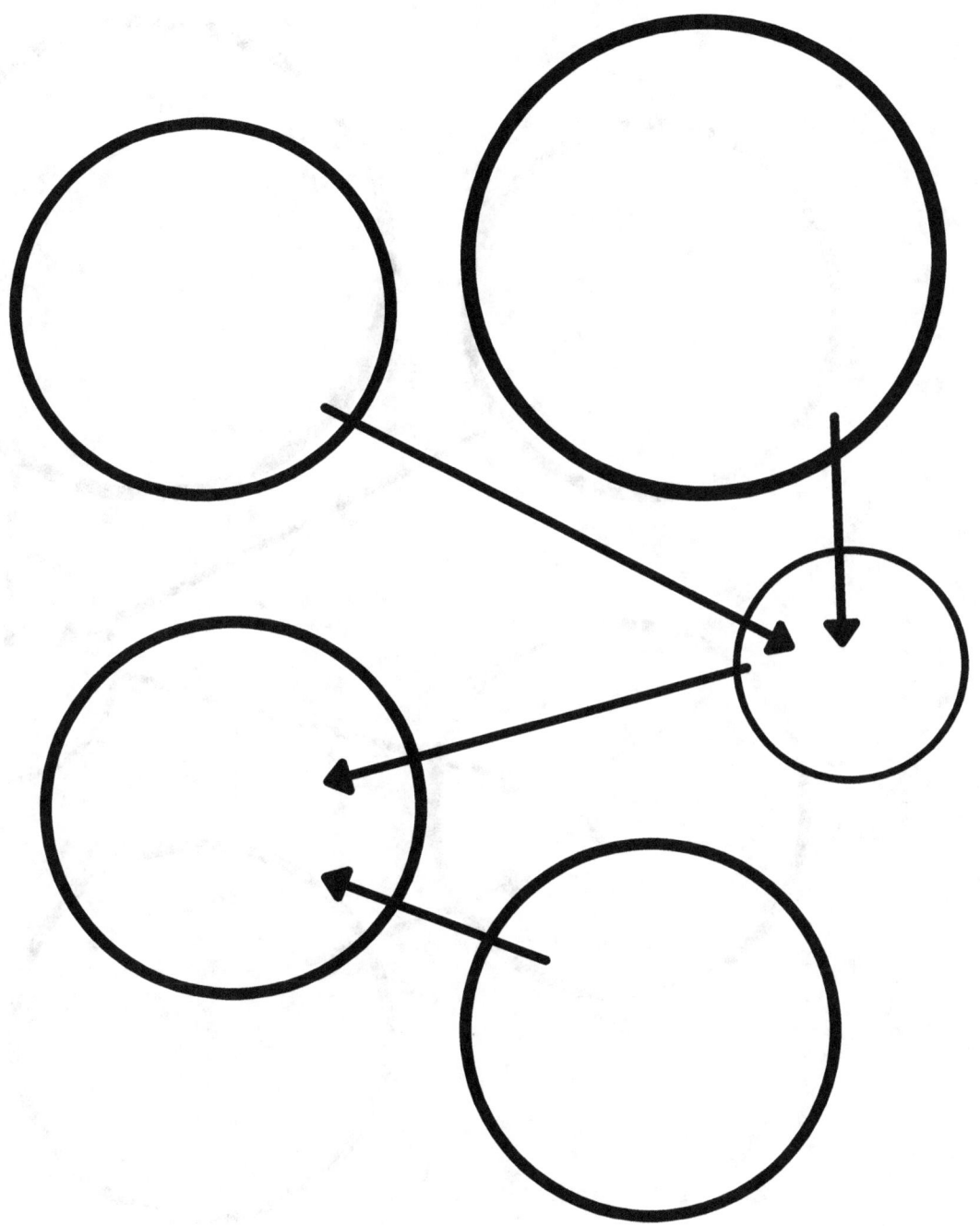

IDEAS

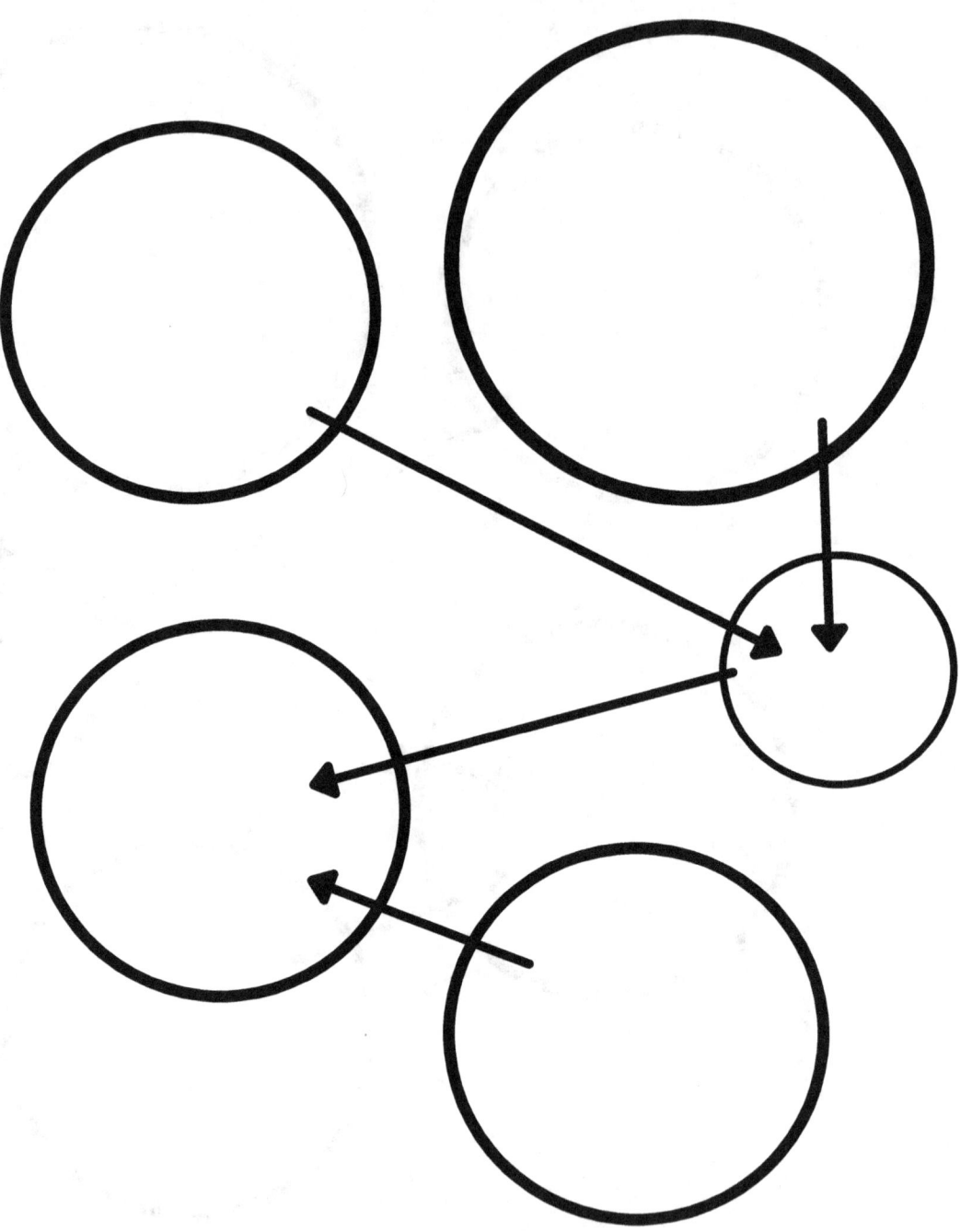

IDEAS

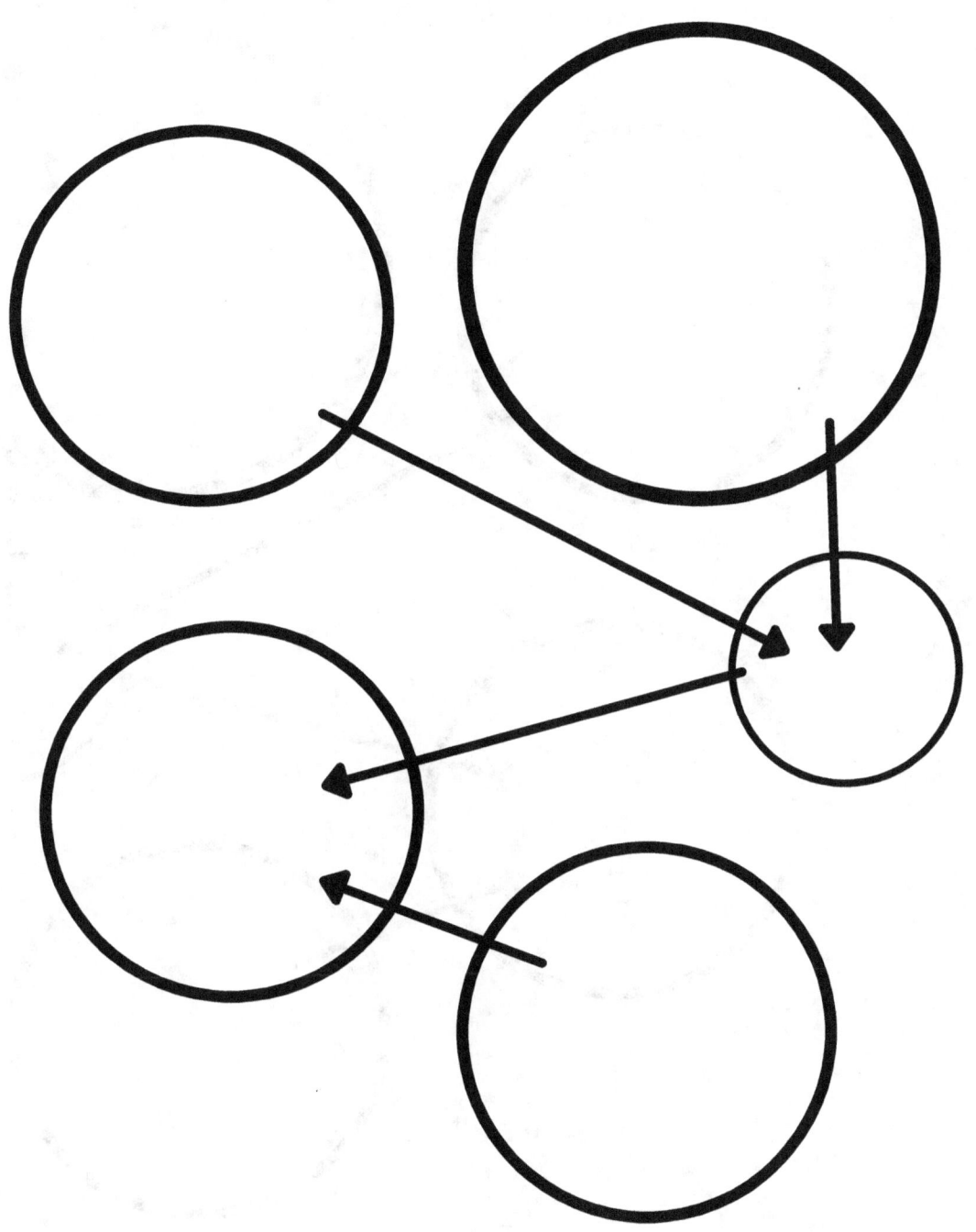

IDEAS

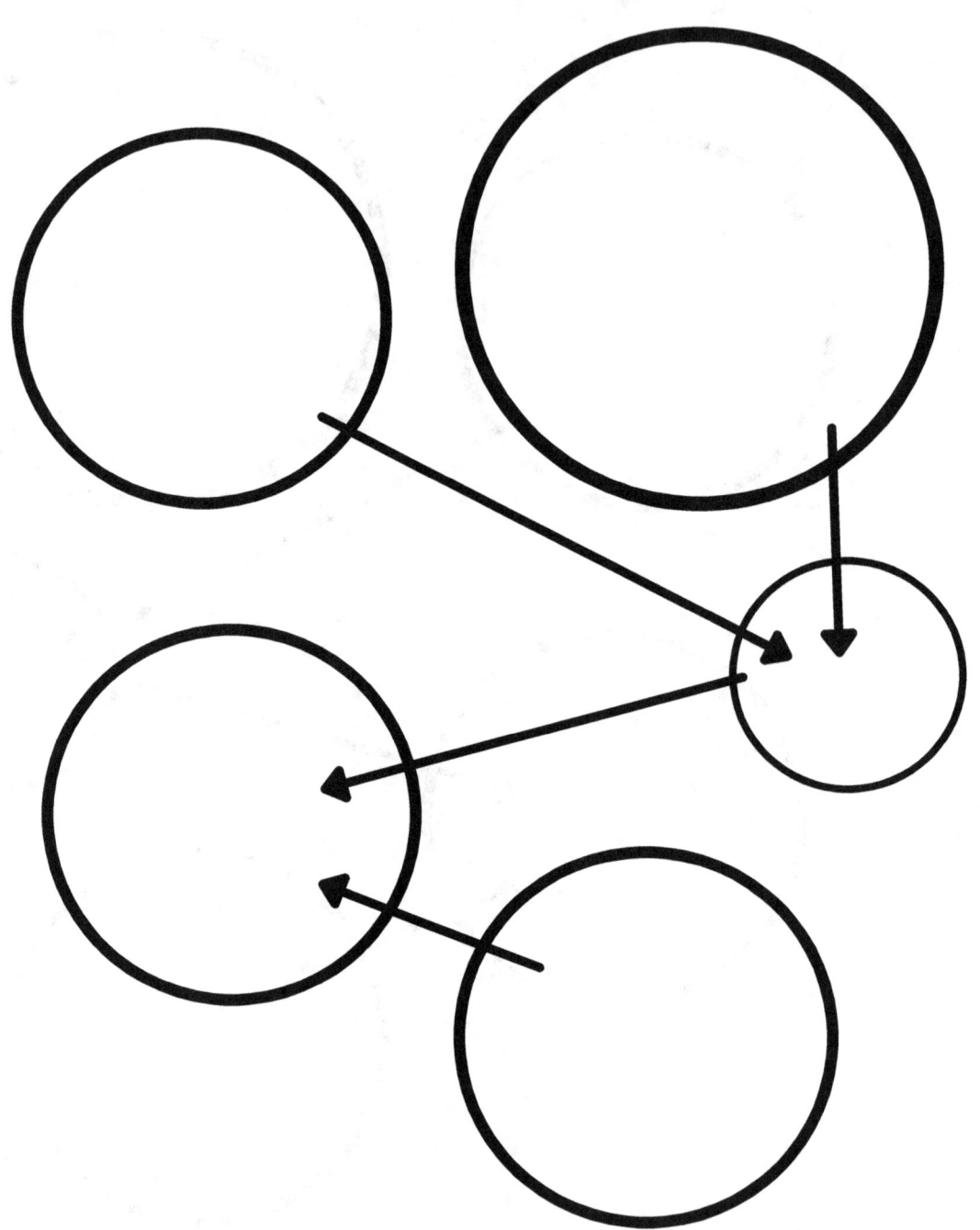

IDEAS

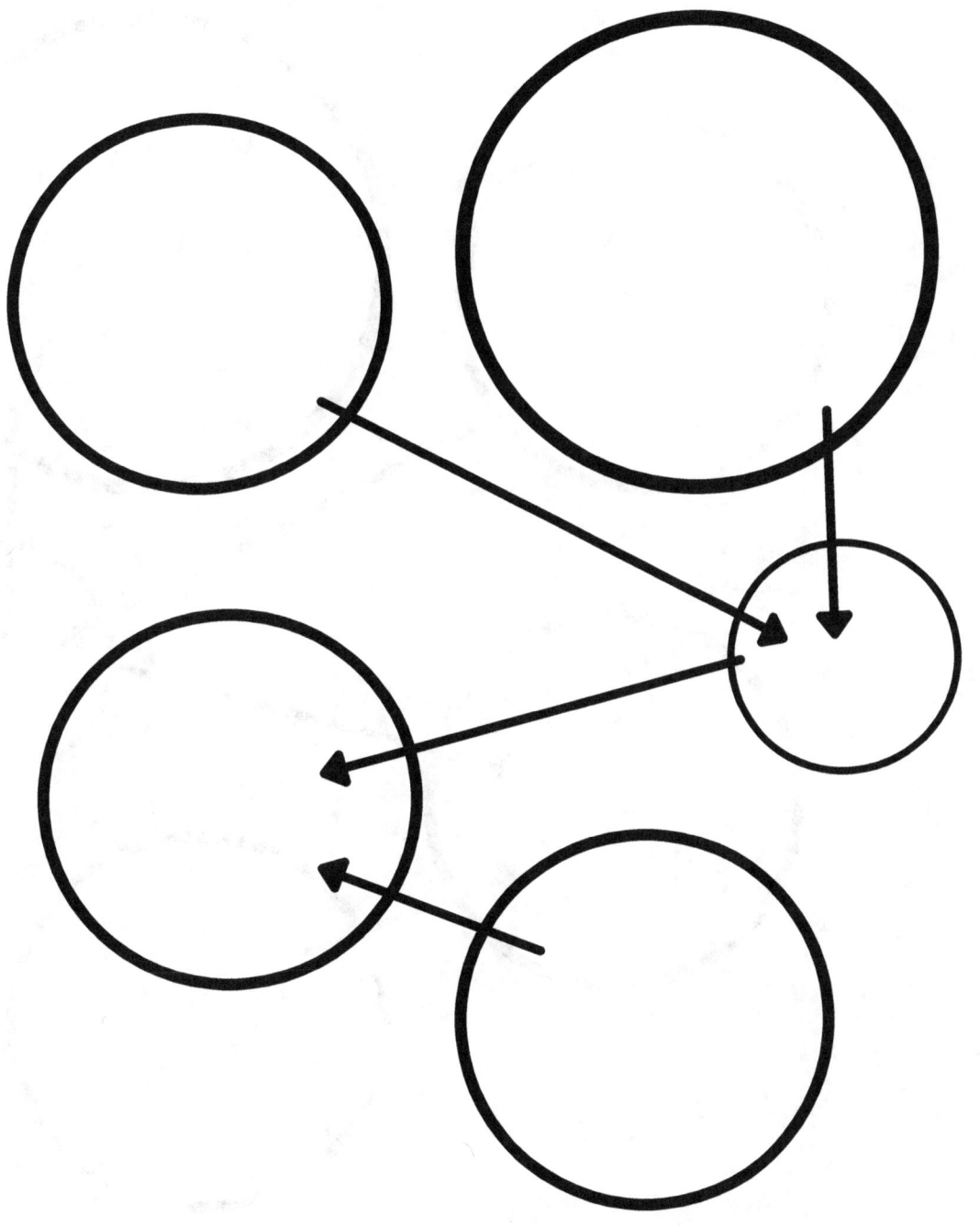

IDEAS

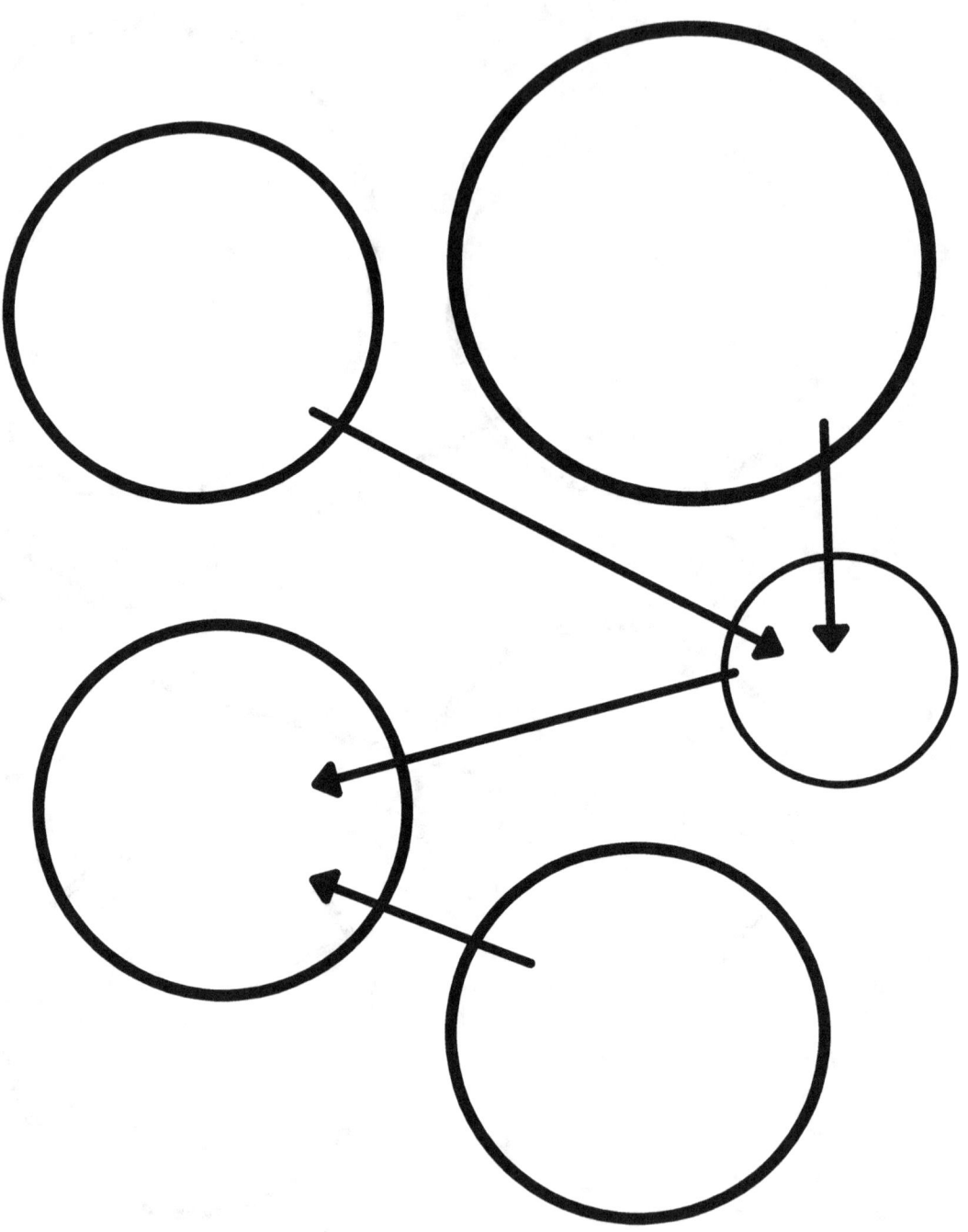

IDEAS

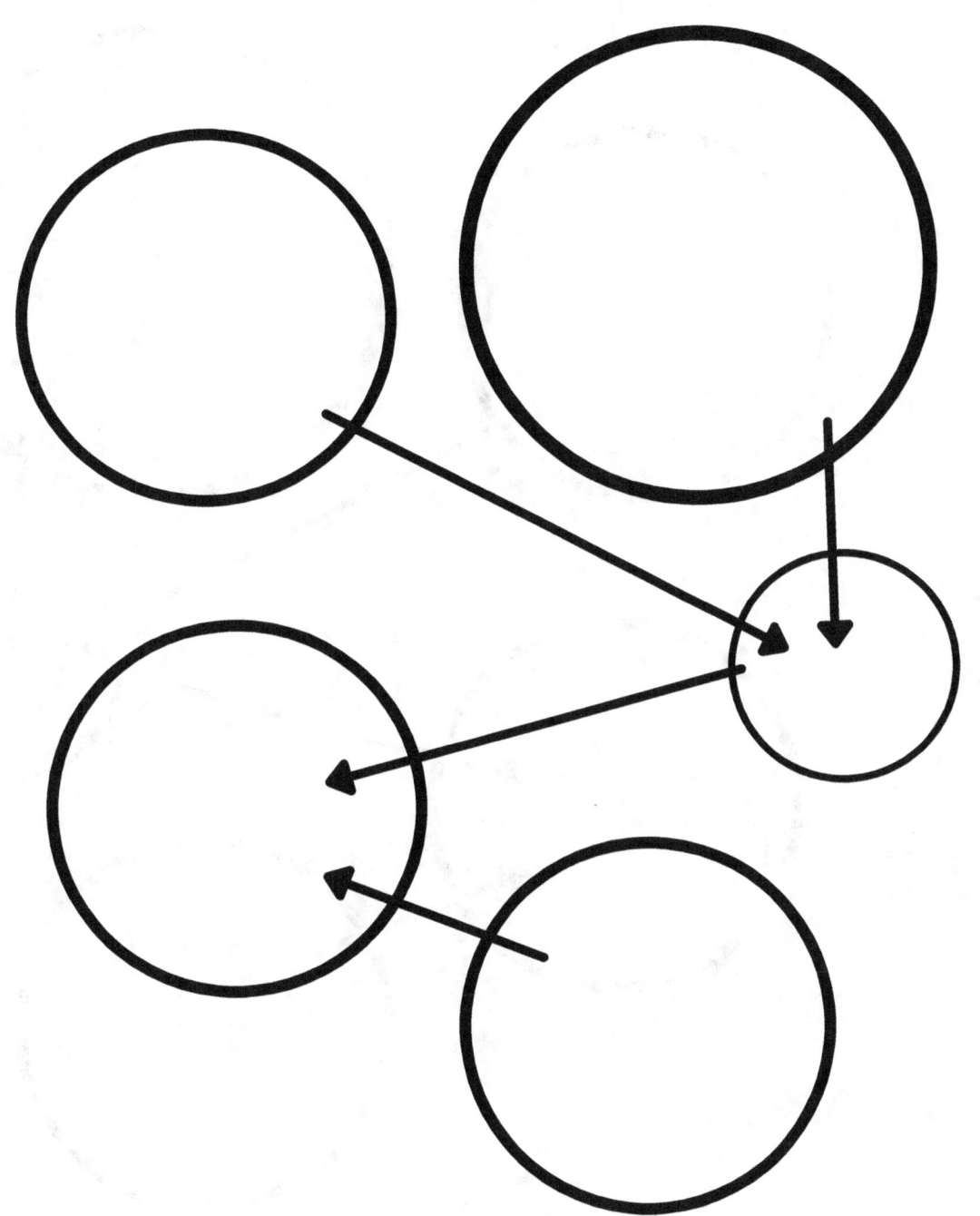

IDEAS

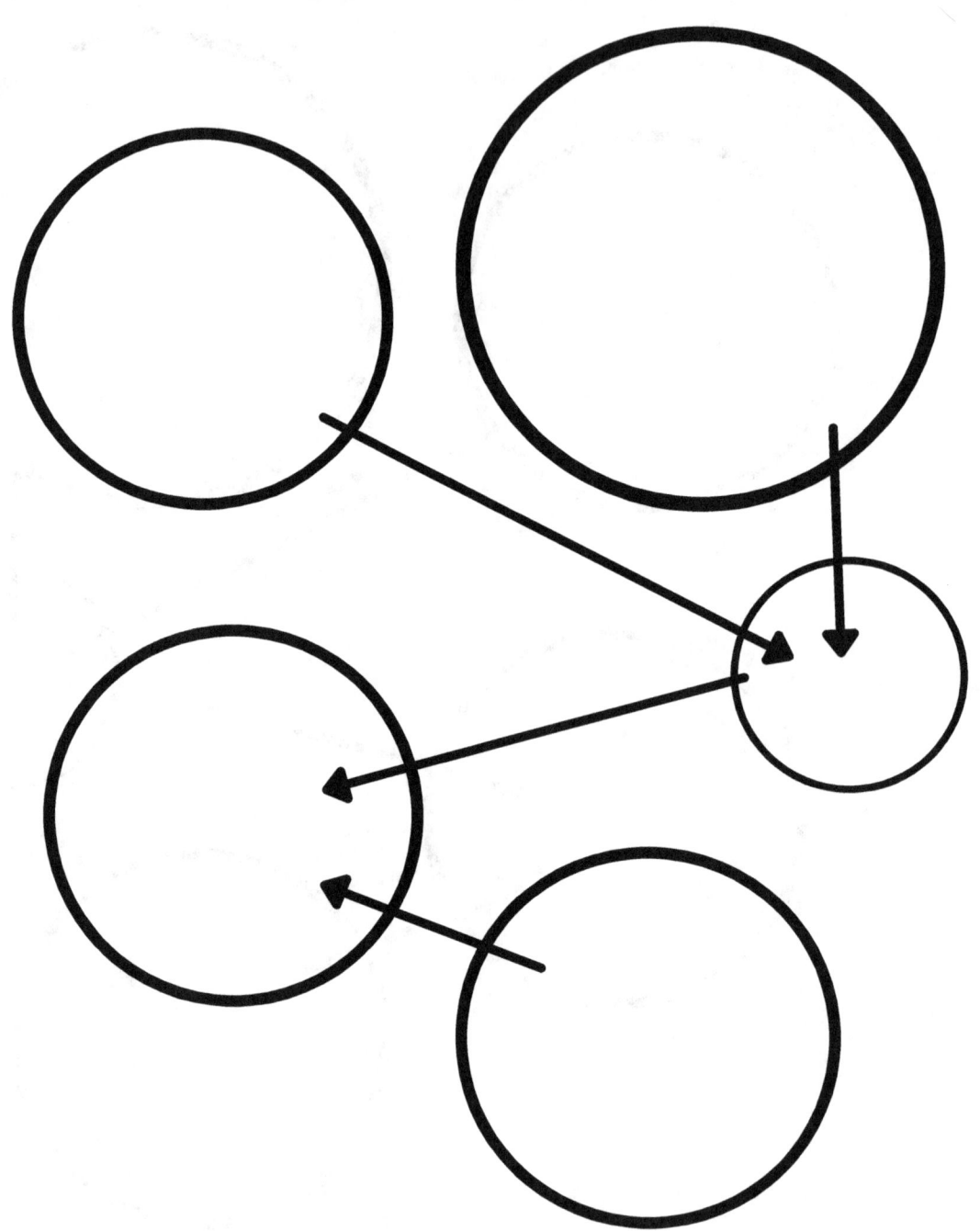

IDEAS

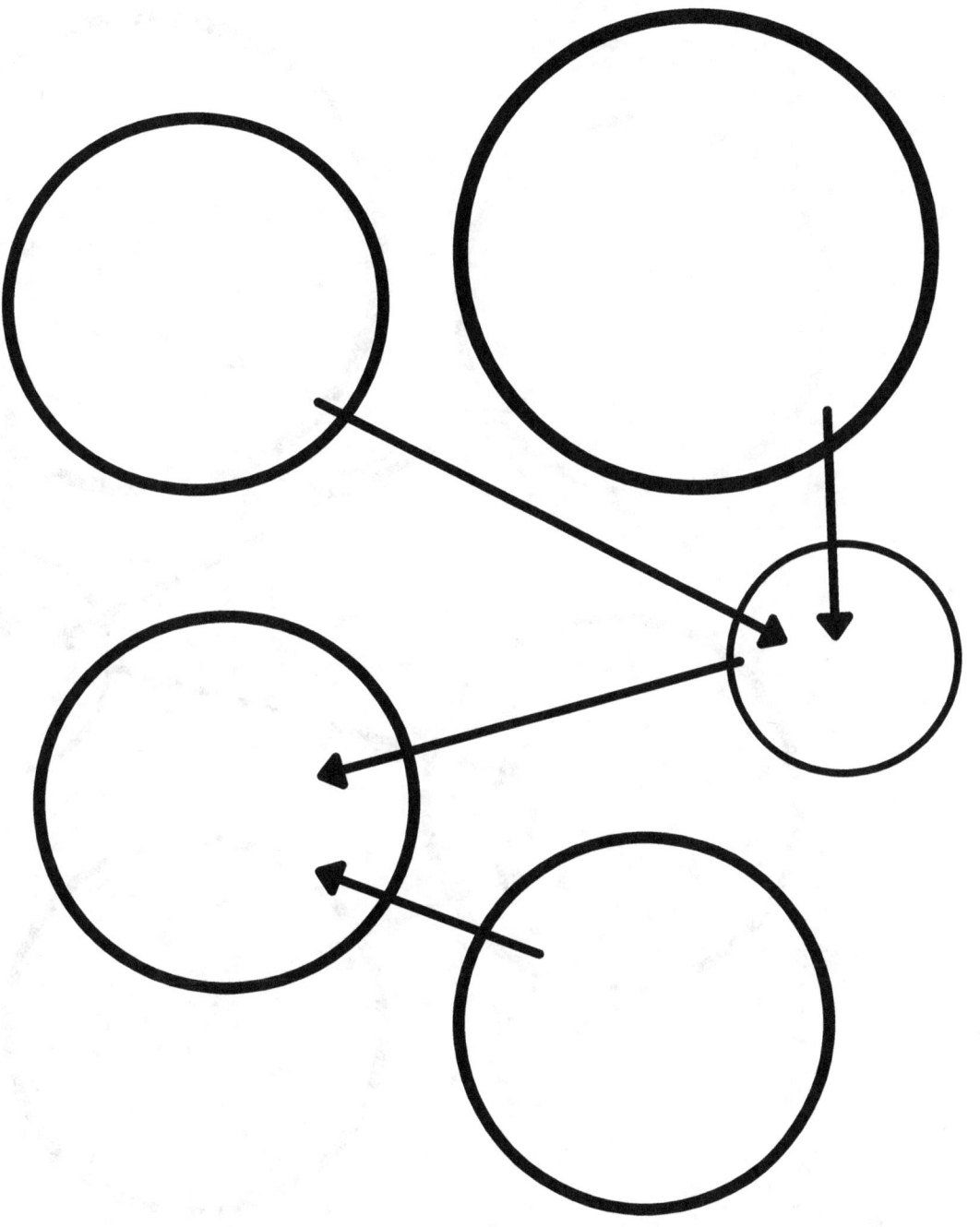

IDEAS

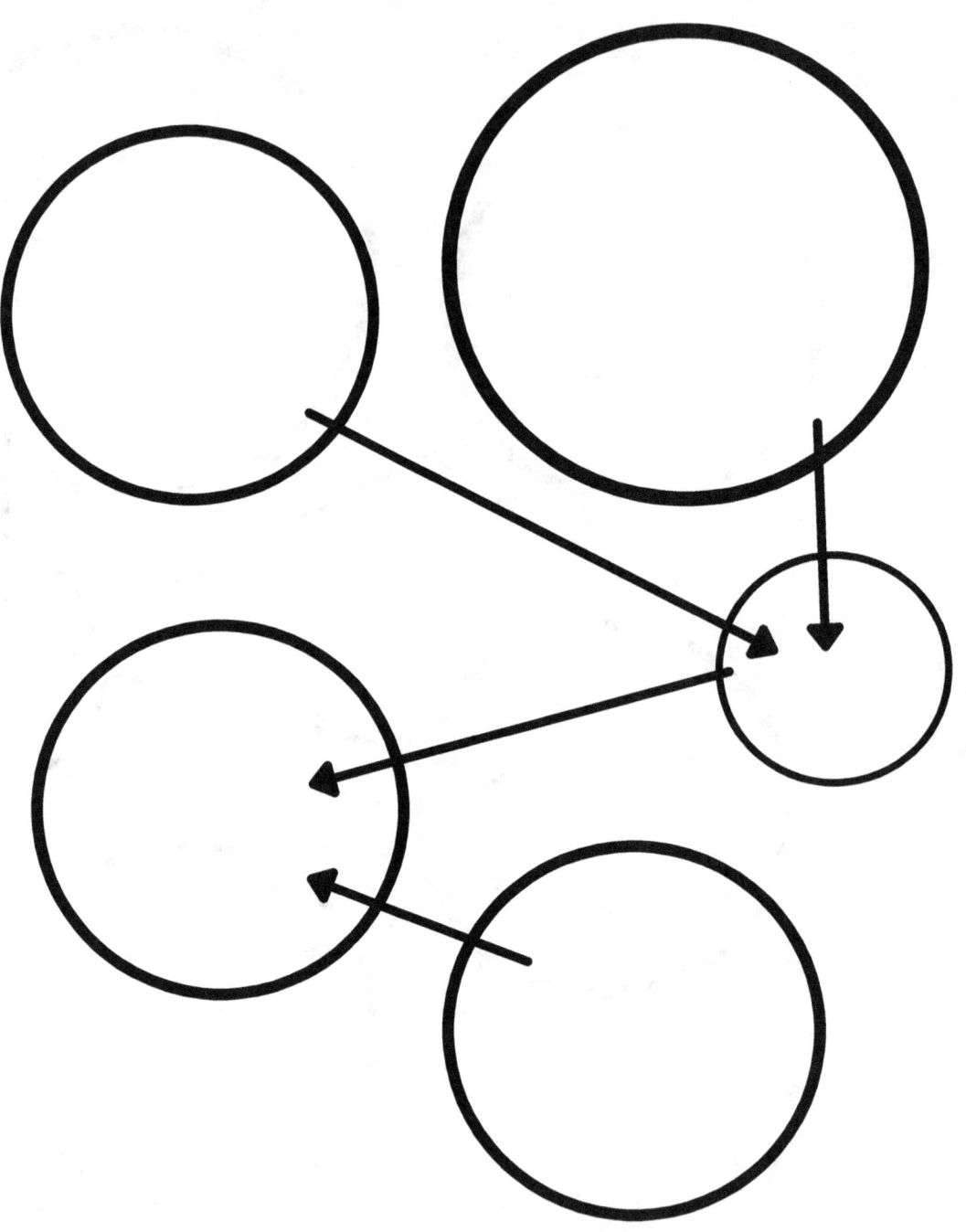

IDEAS

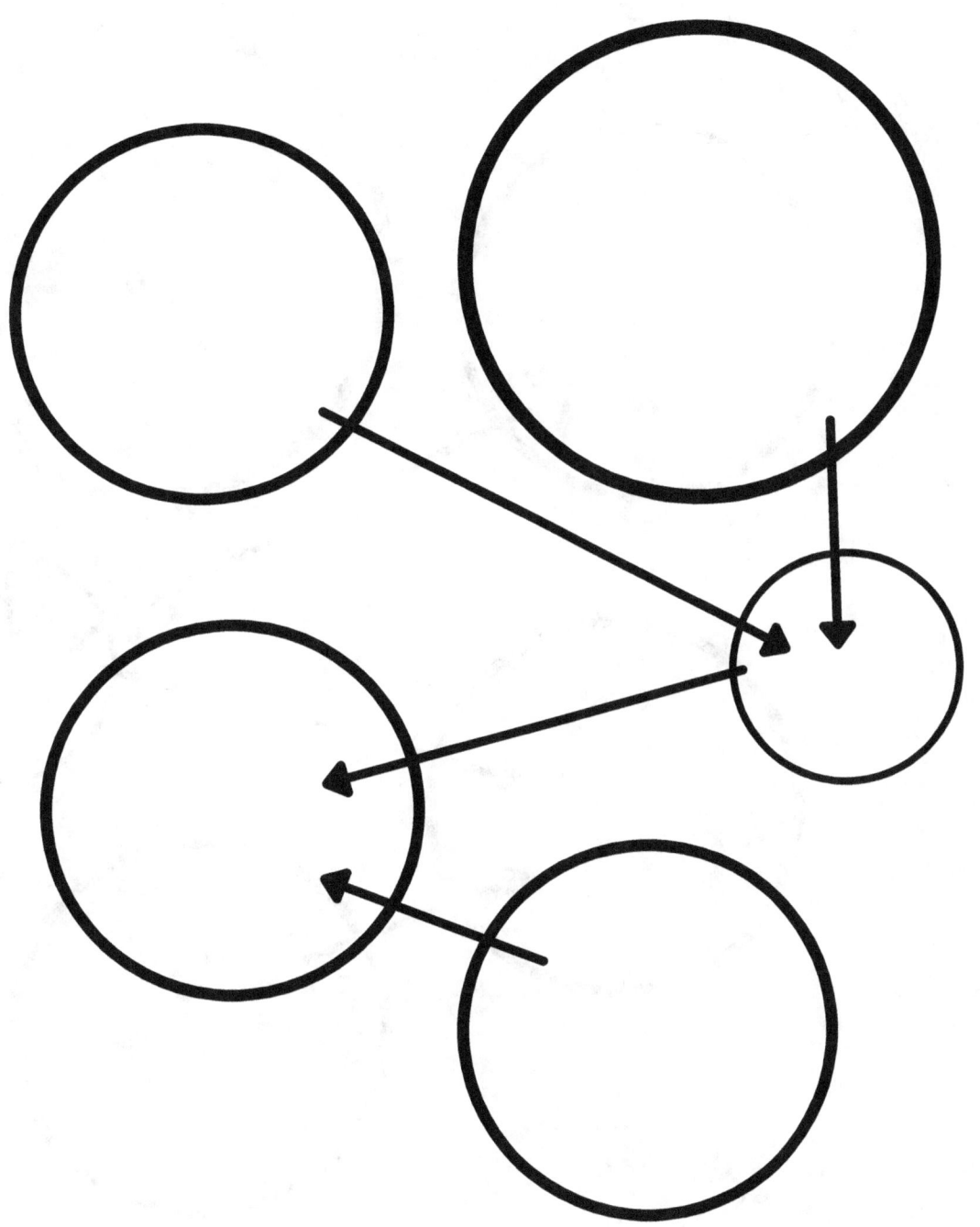

IDEAS

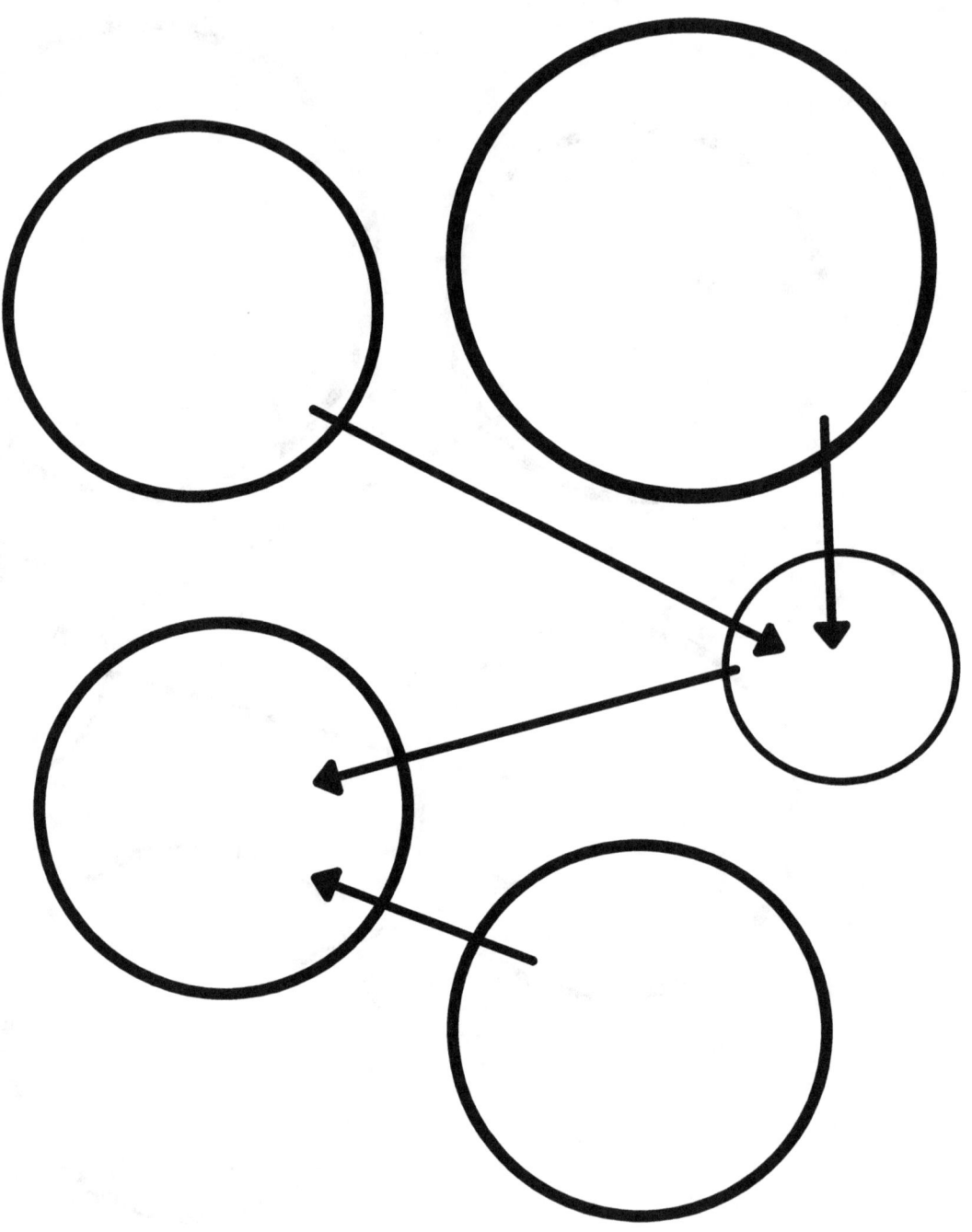

IDEAS

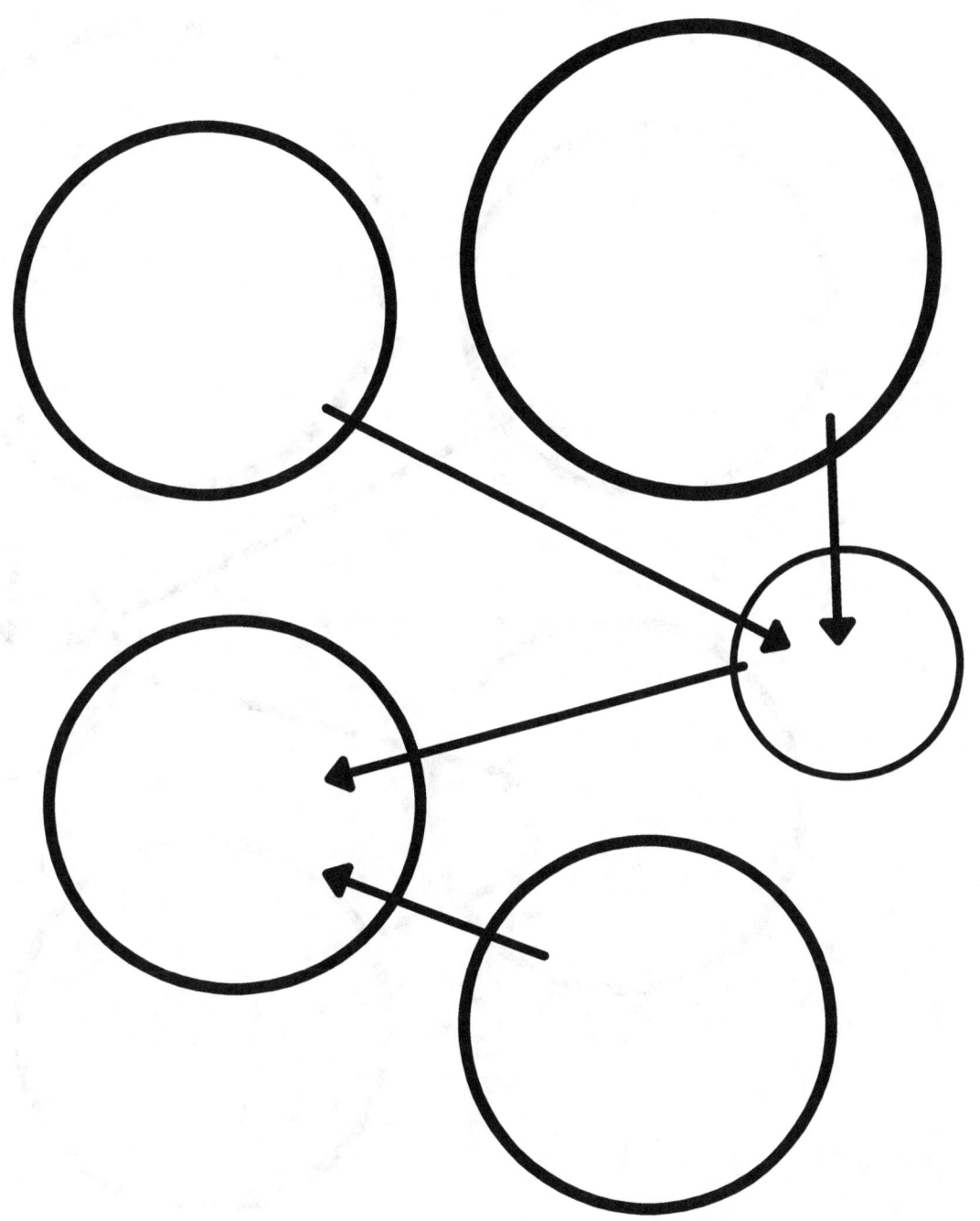

IDEAS

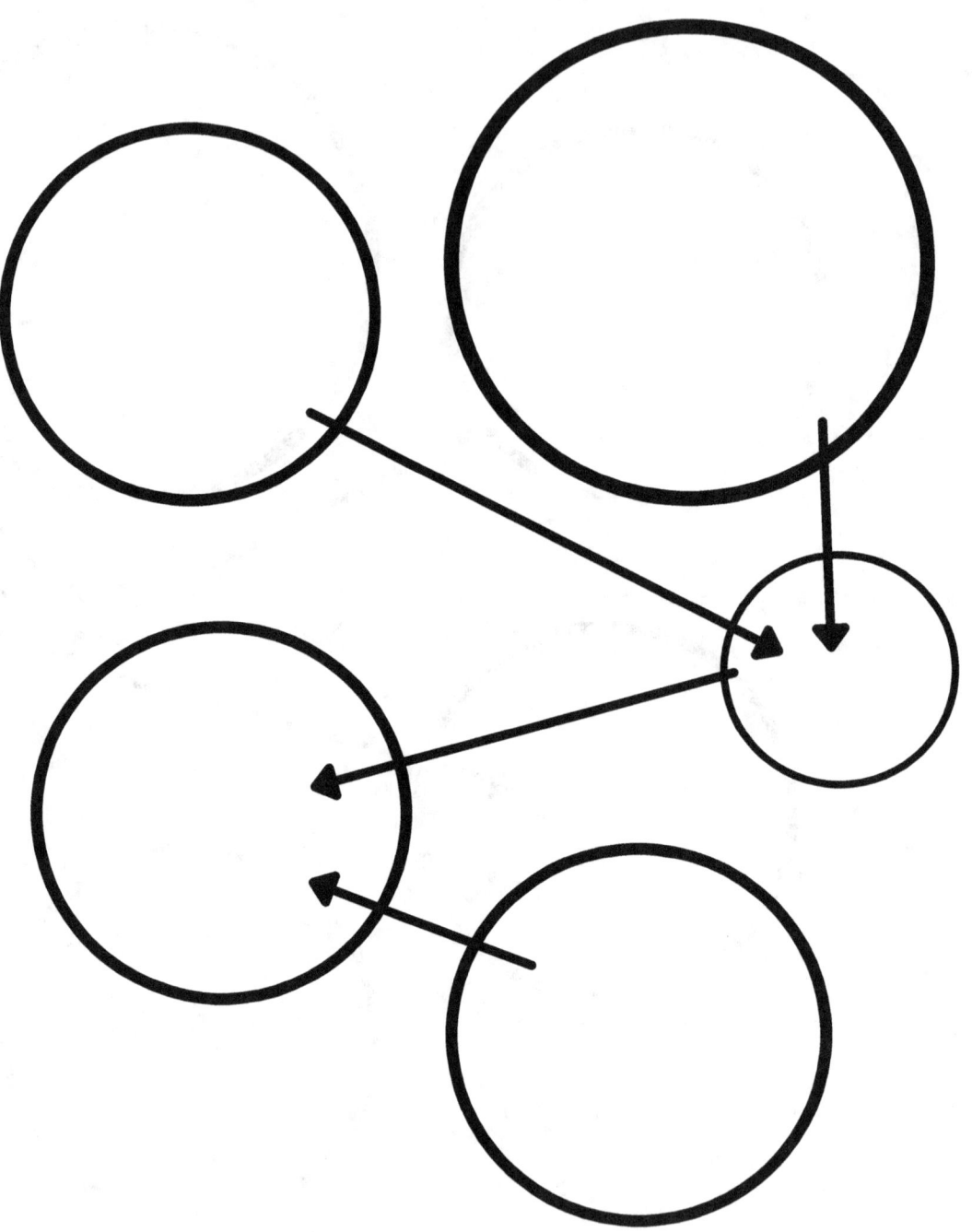

IDEAS

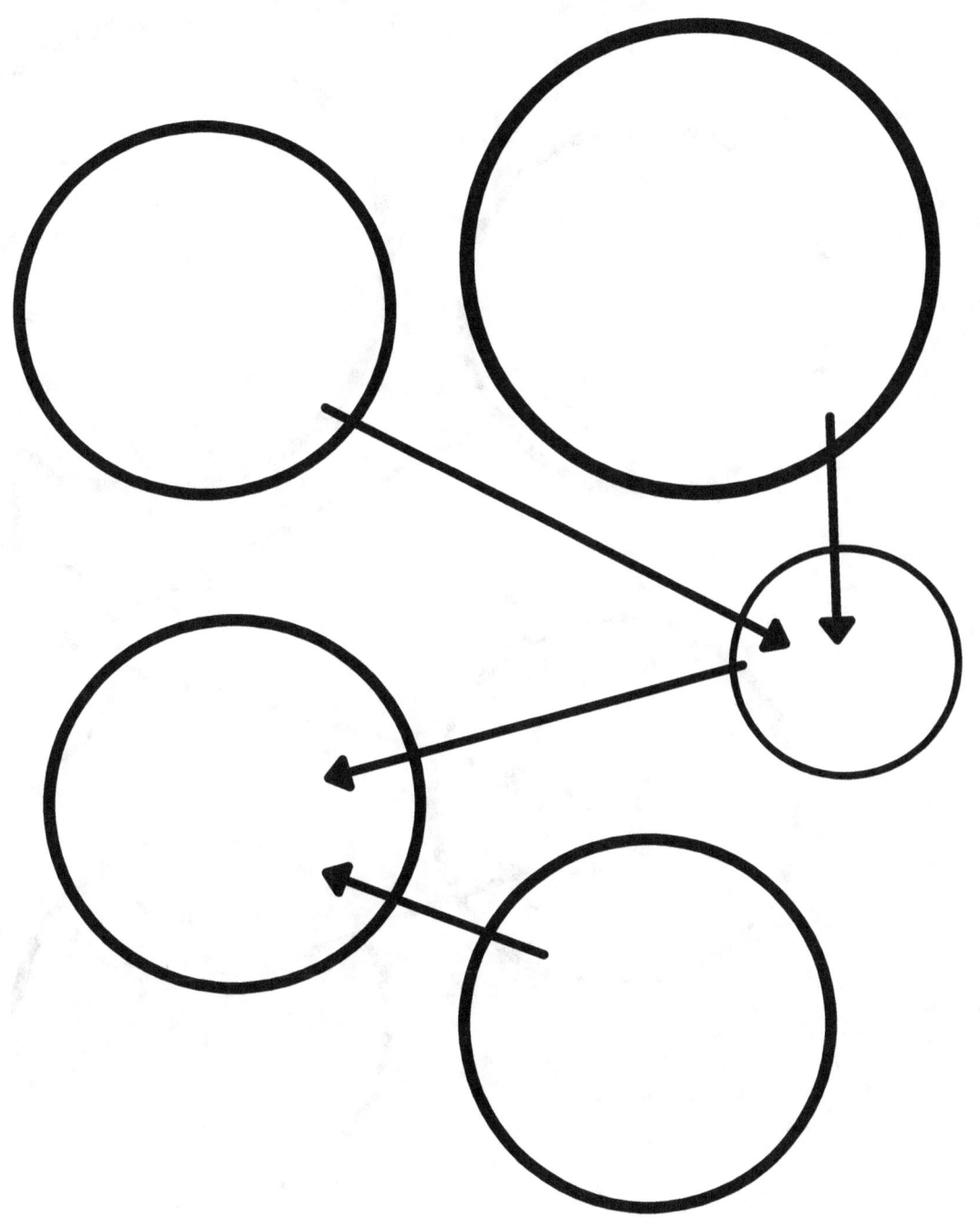

IDEAS

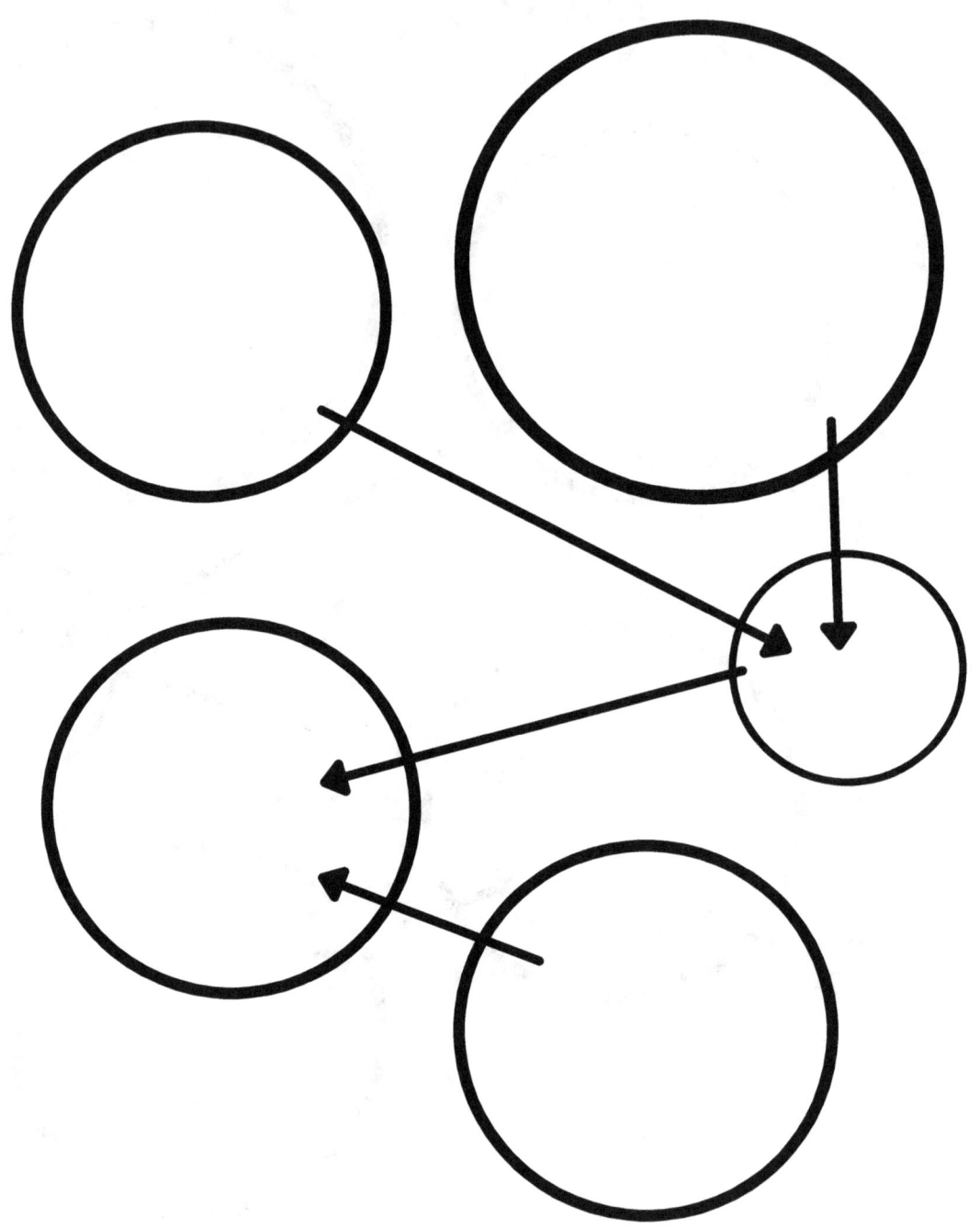

IDEAS

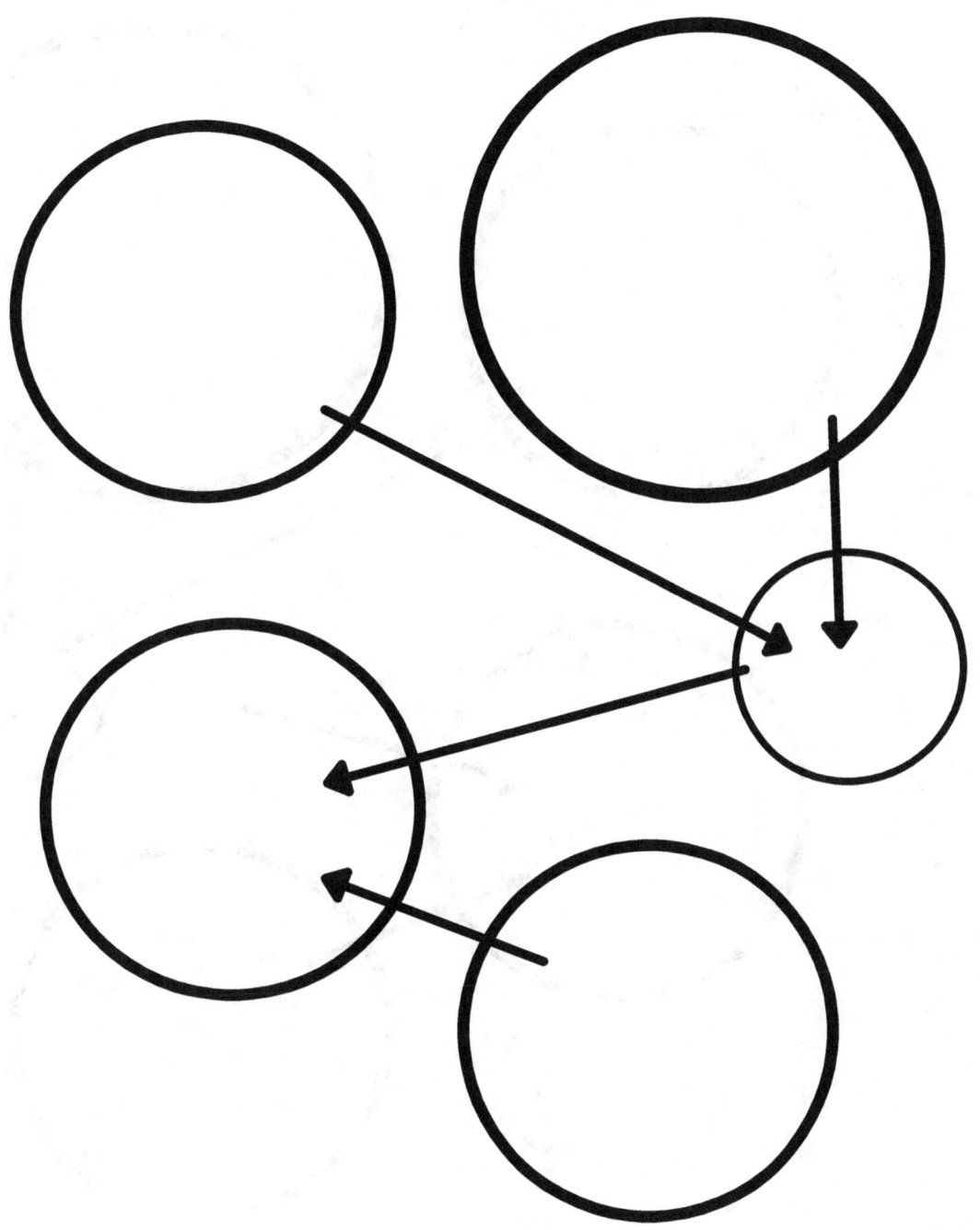

IDEAS

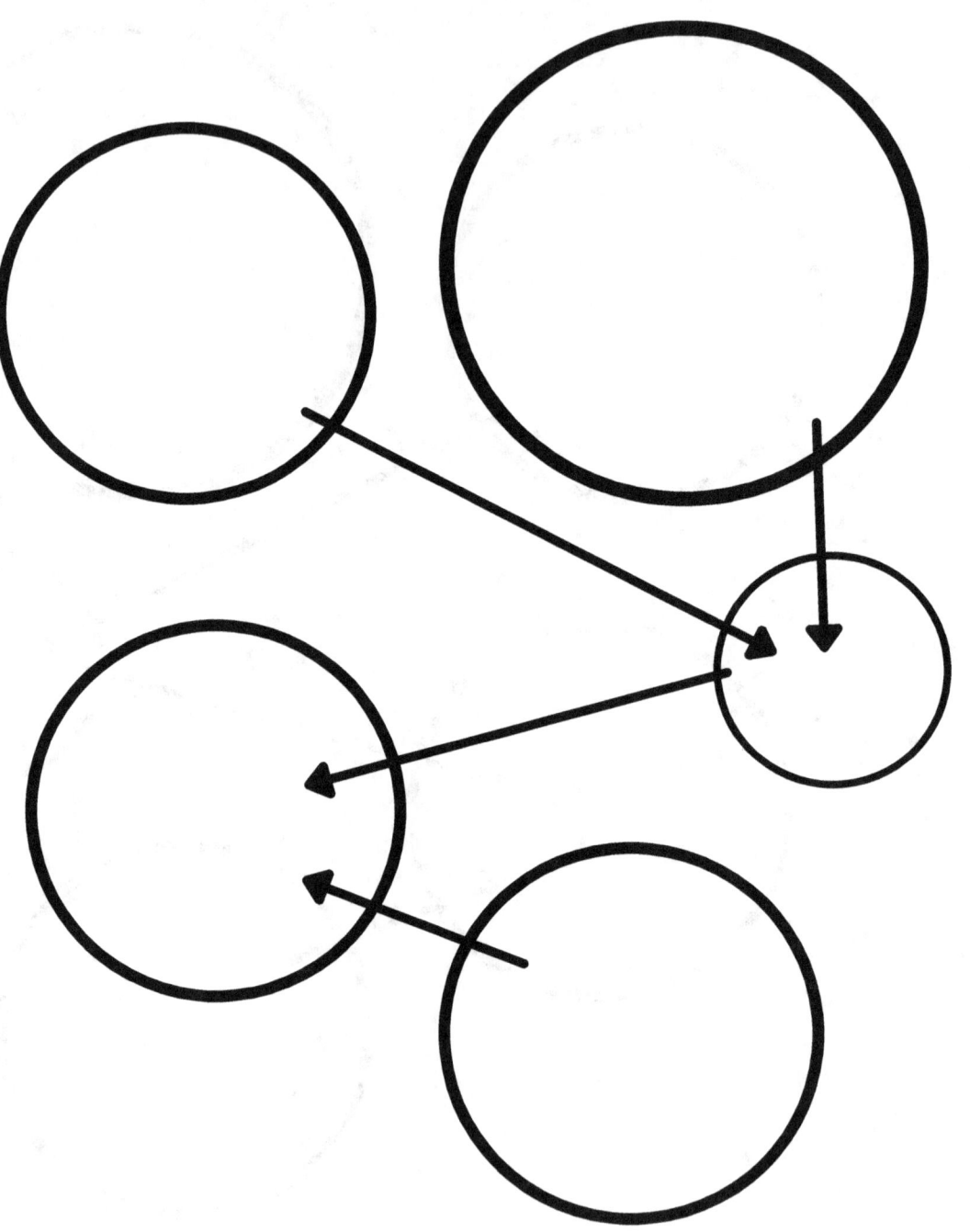

IDEAS

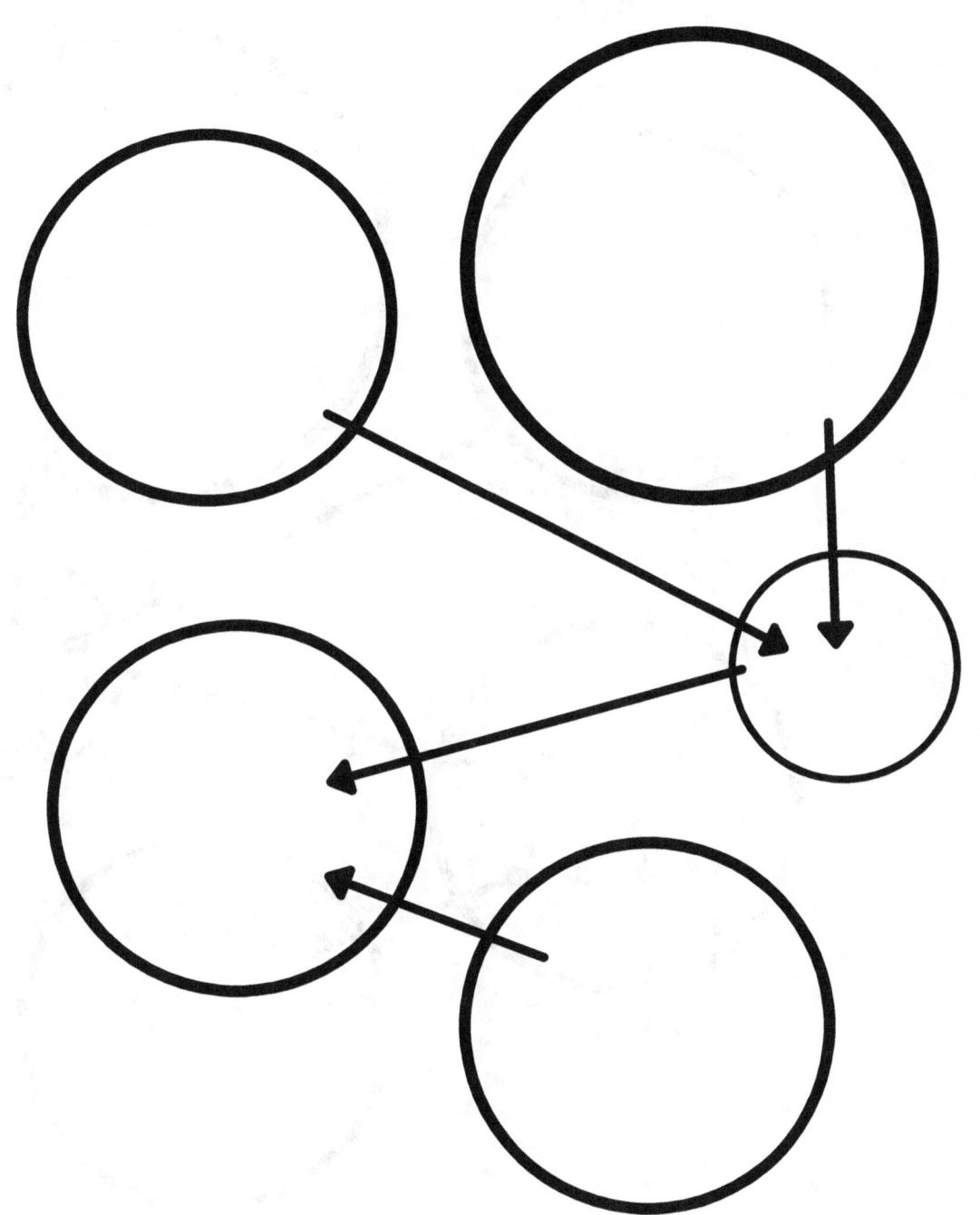

IDEAS

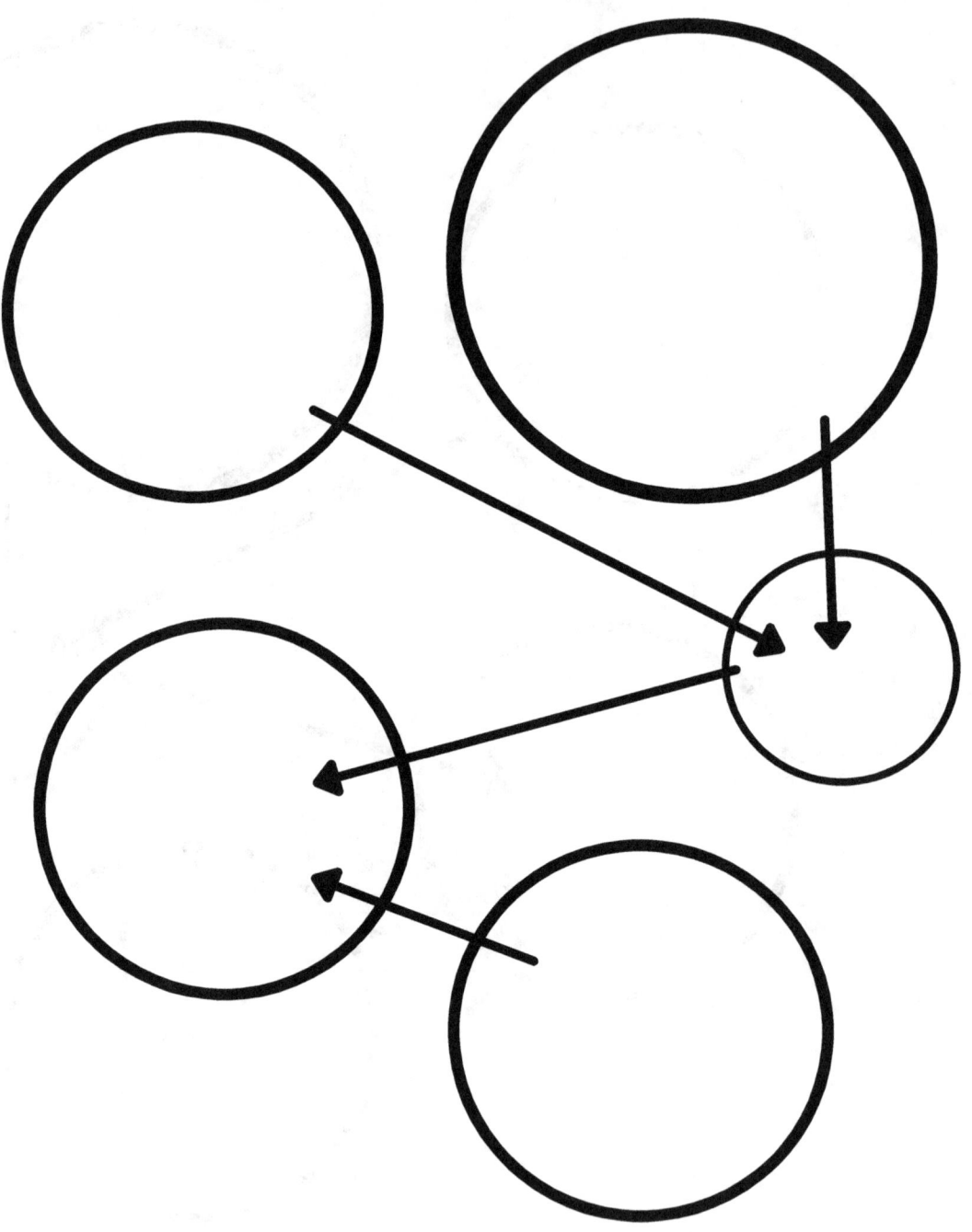

IDEAS

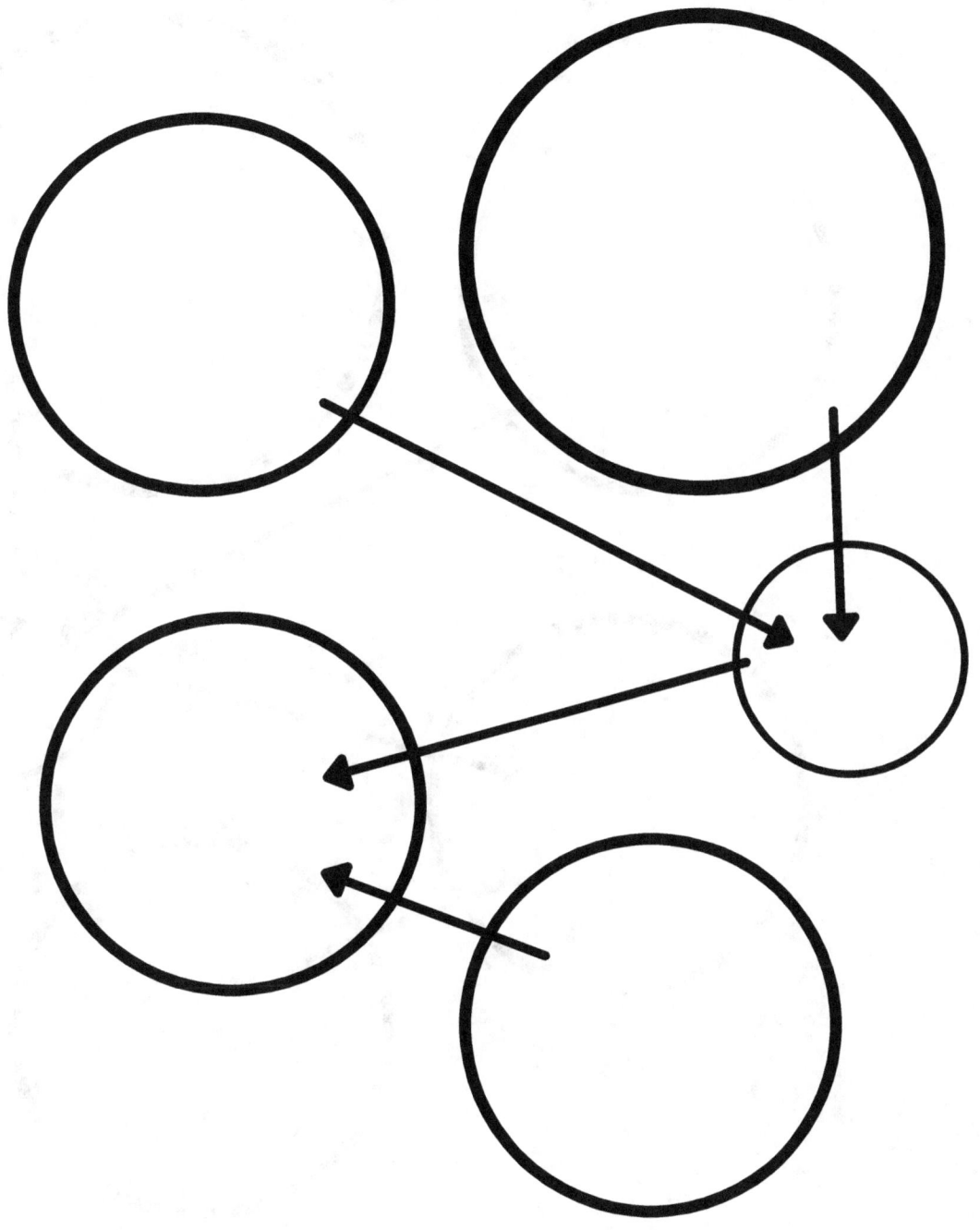

IDEAS

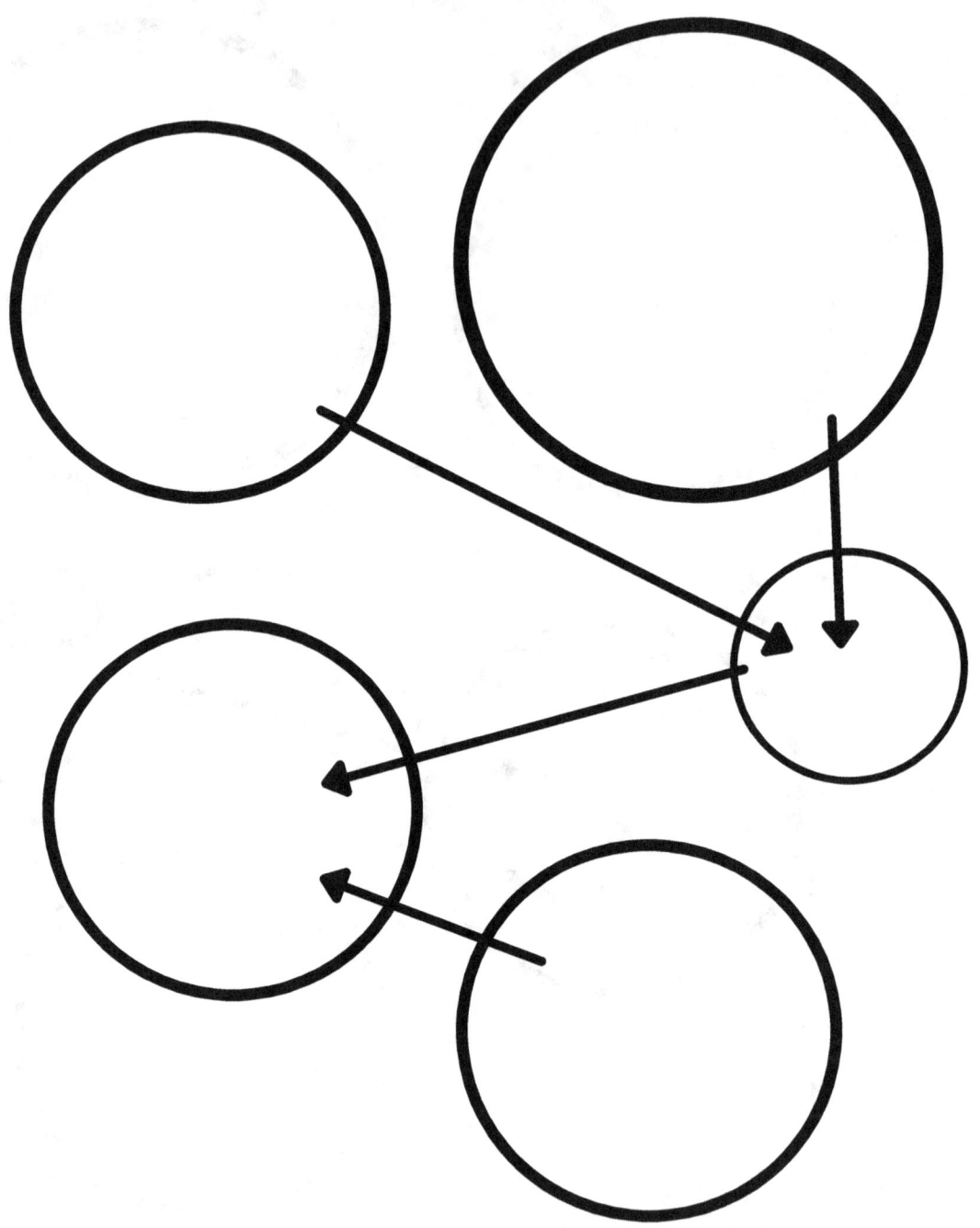

IDEAS

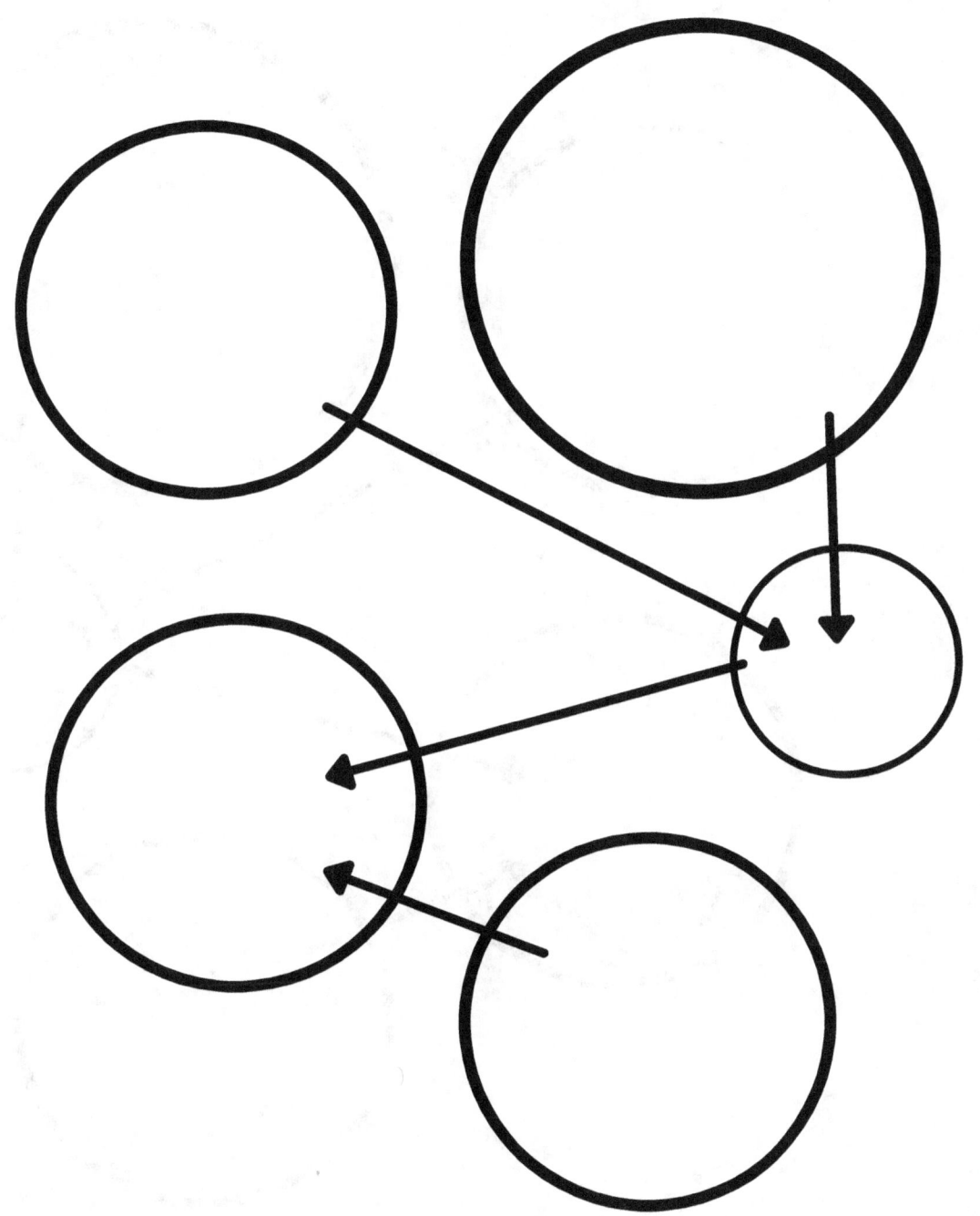

IDEAS

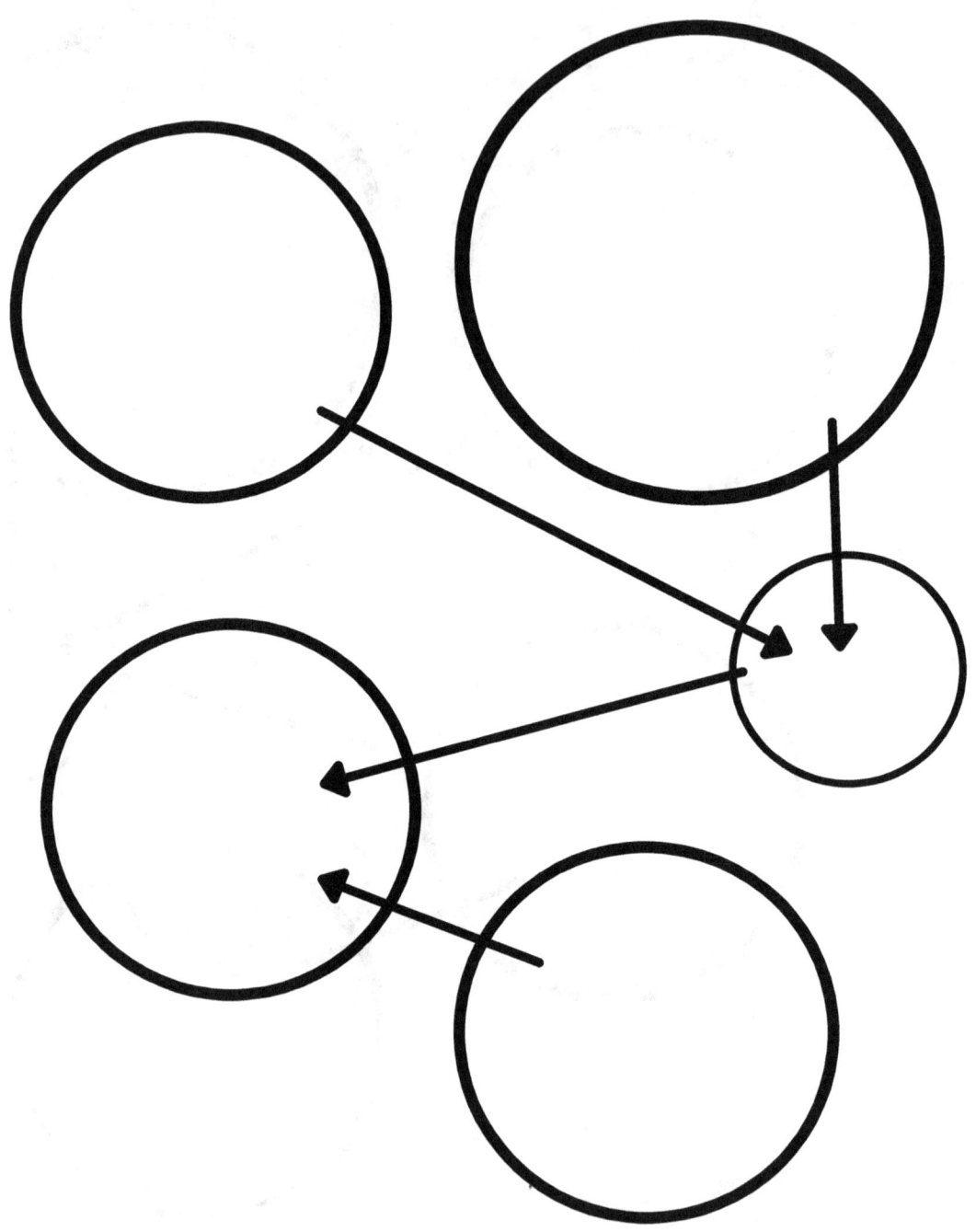

IDEAS

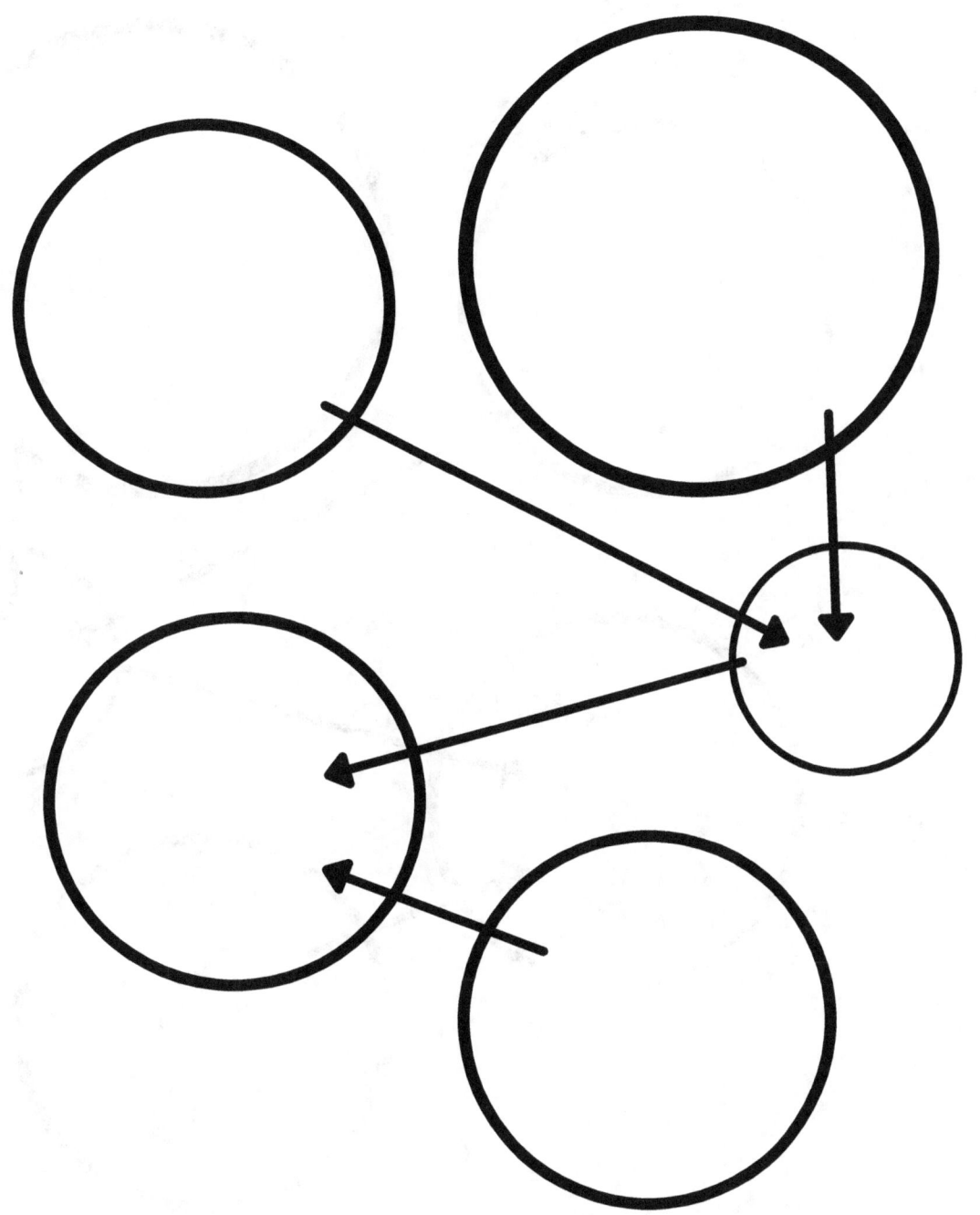

IDEAS

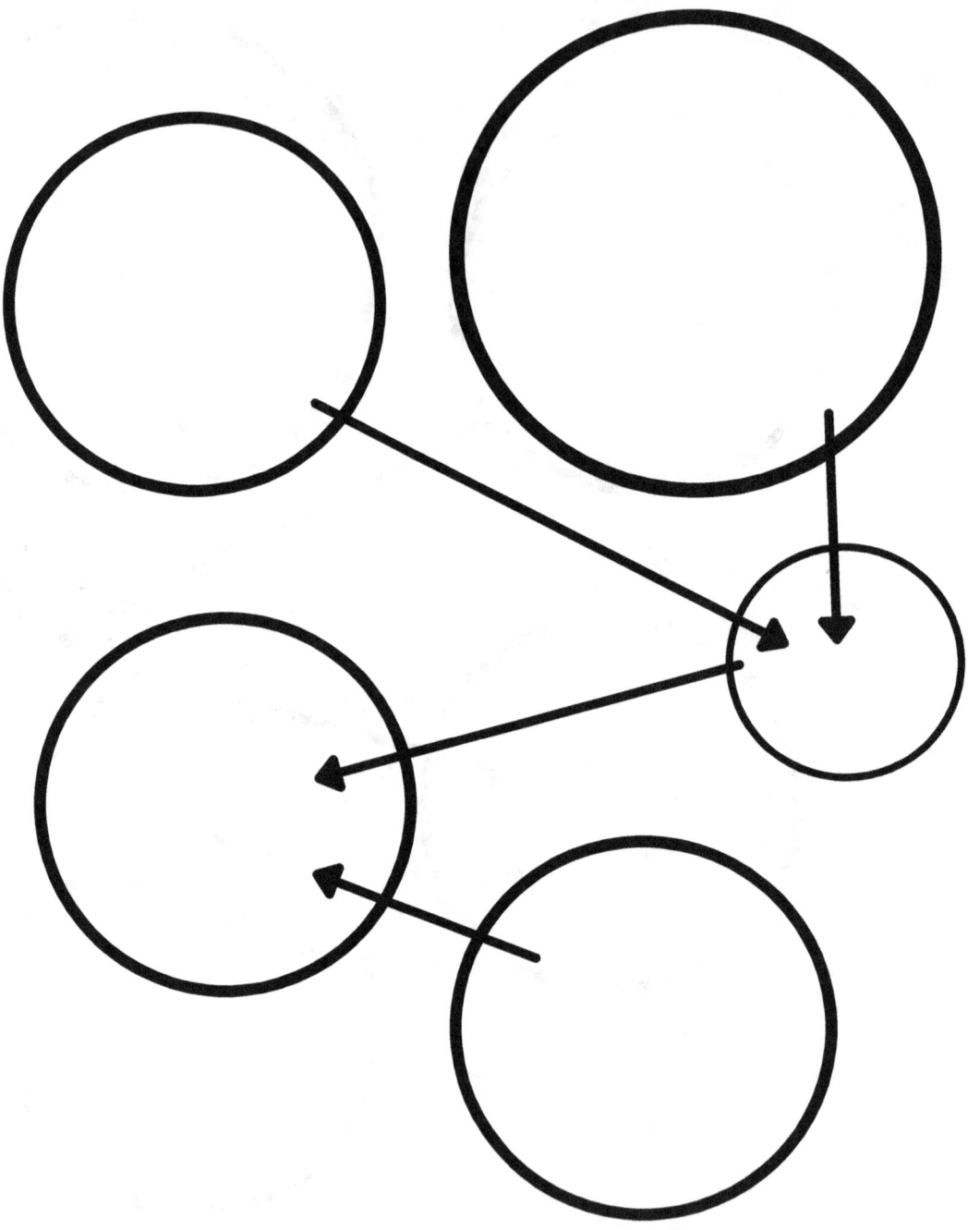

IDEAS

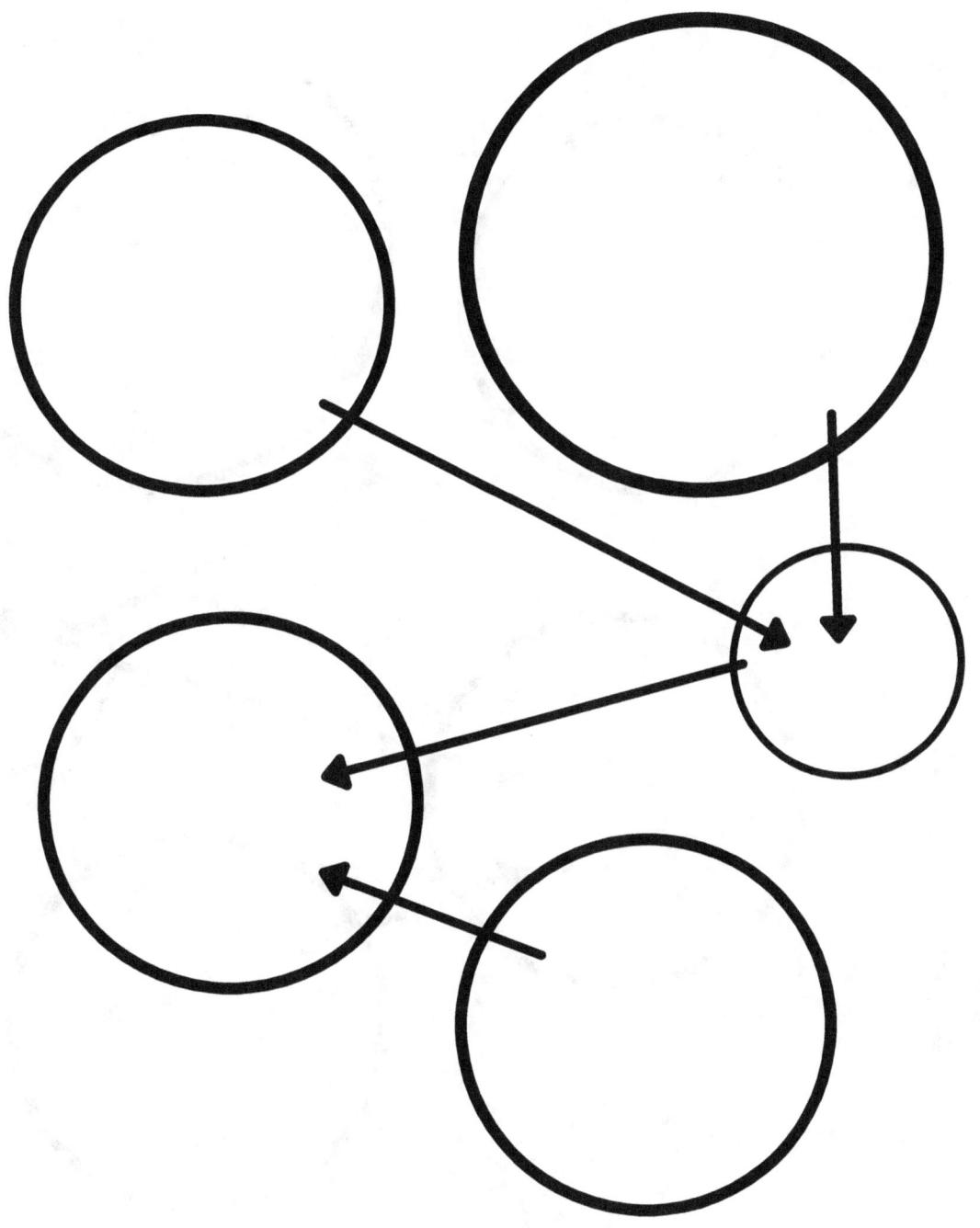

IDEAS

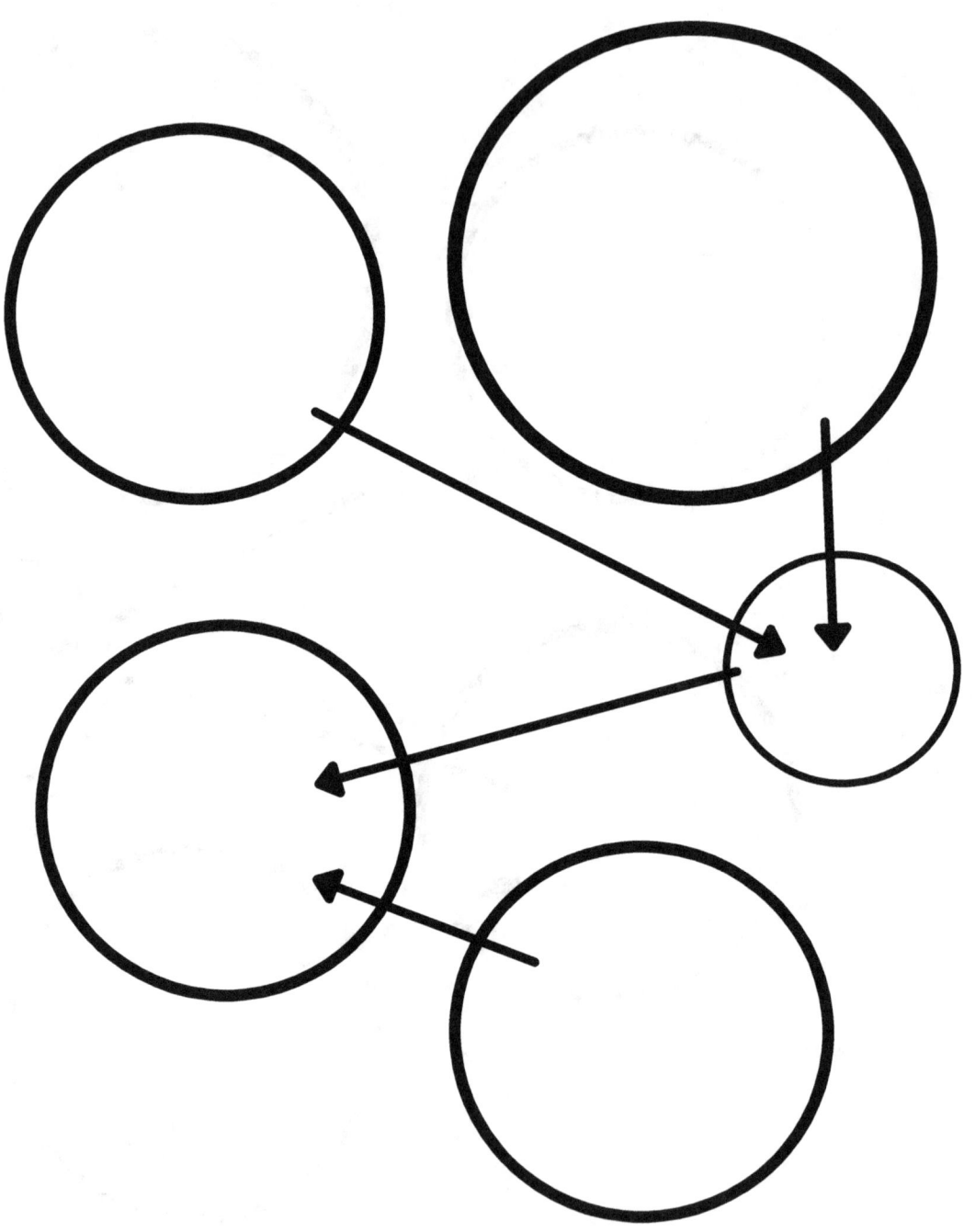

IDEAS

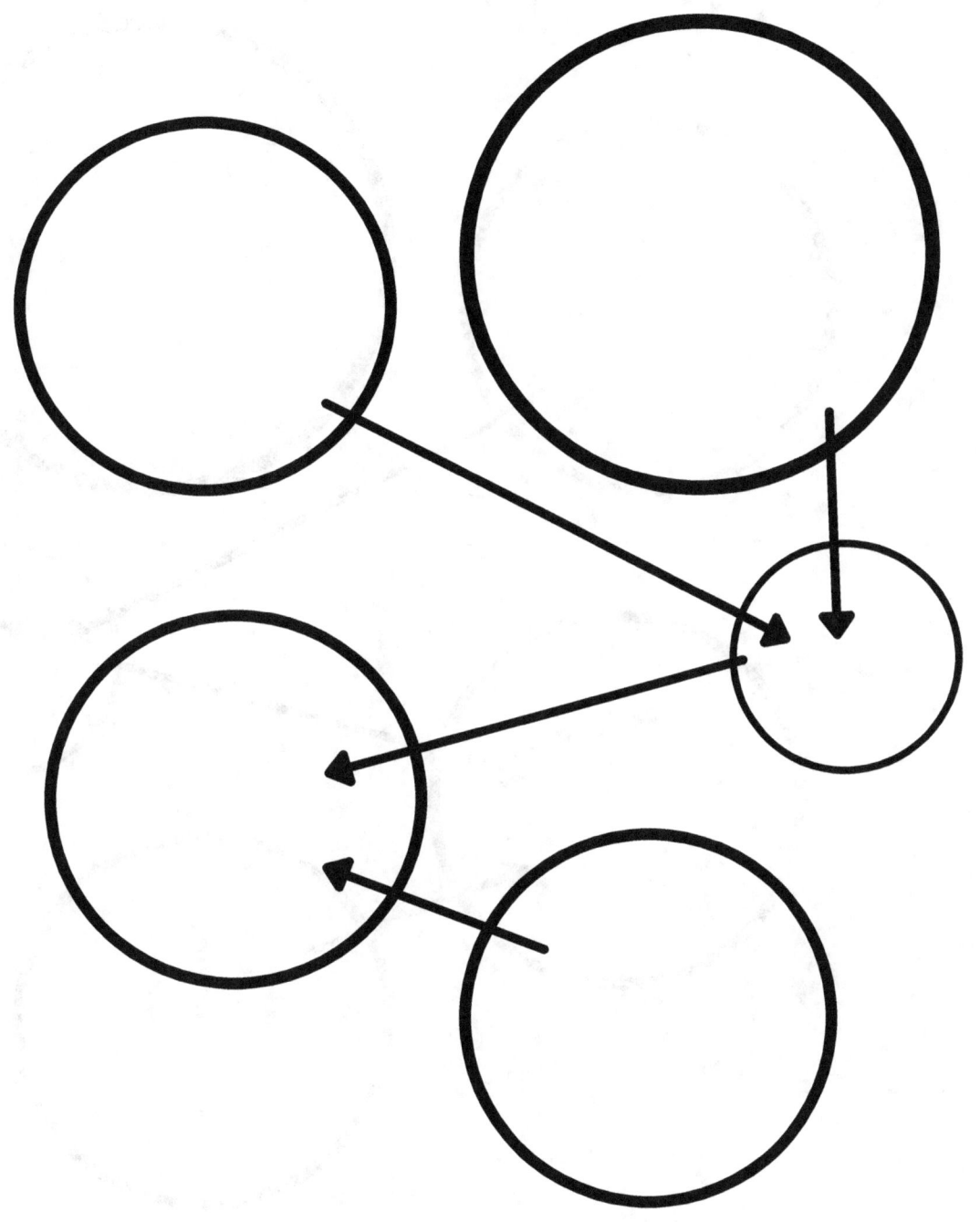

IDEAS

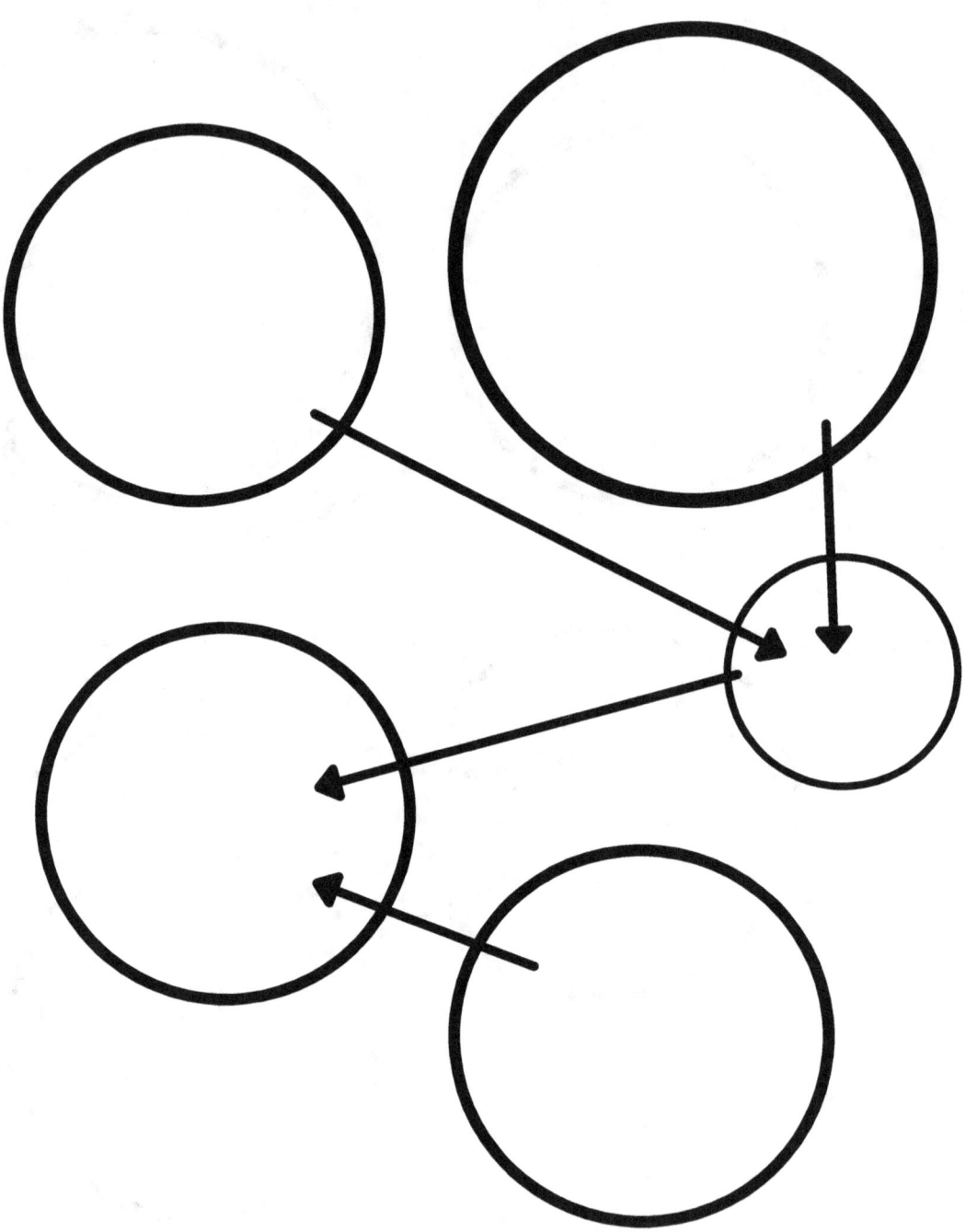

IDEAS

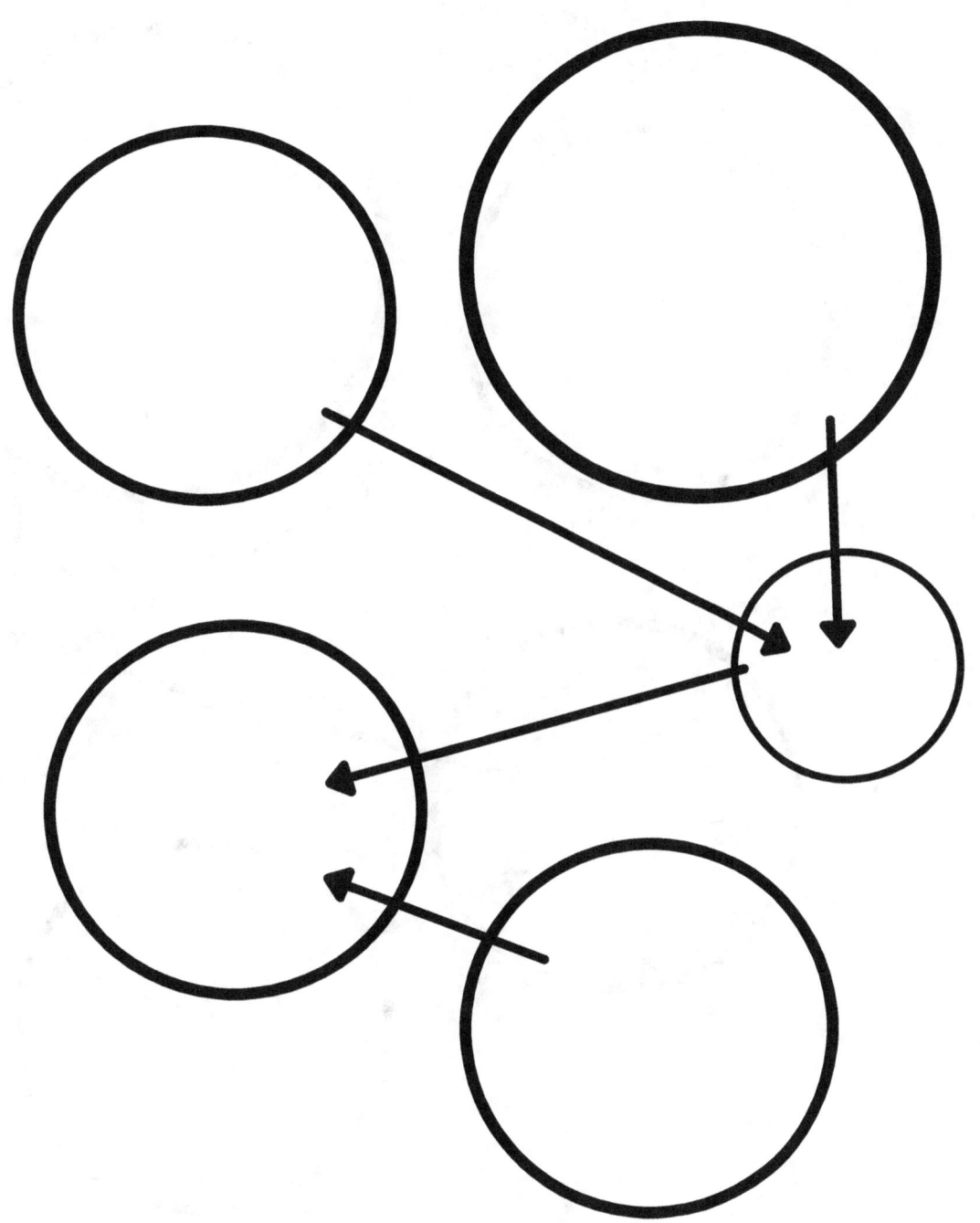

IDEAS

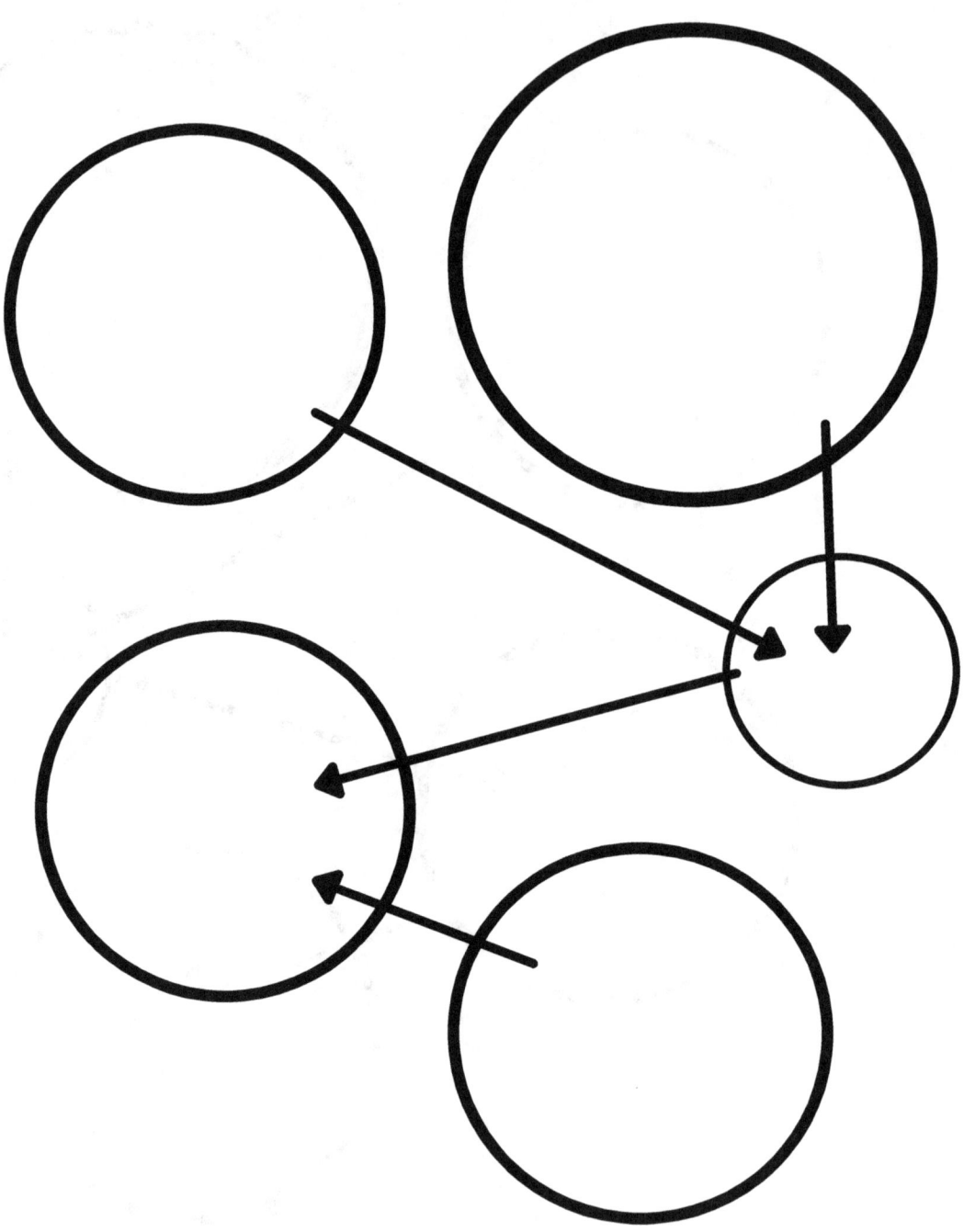

IDEAS

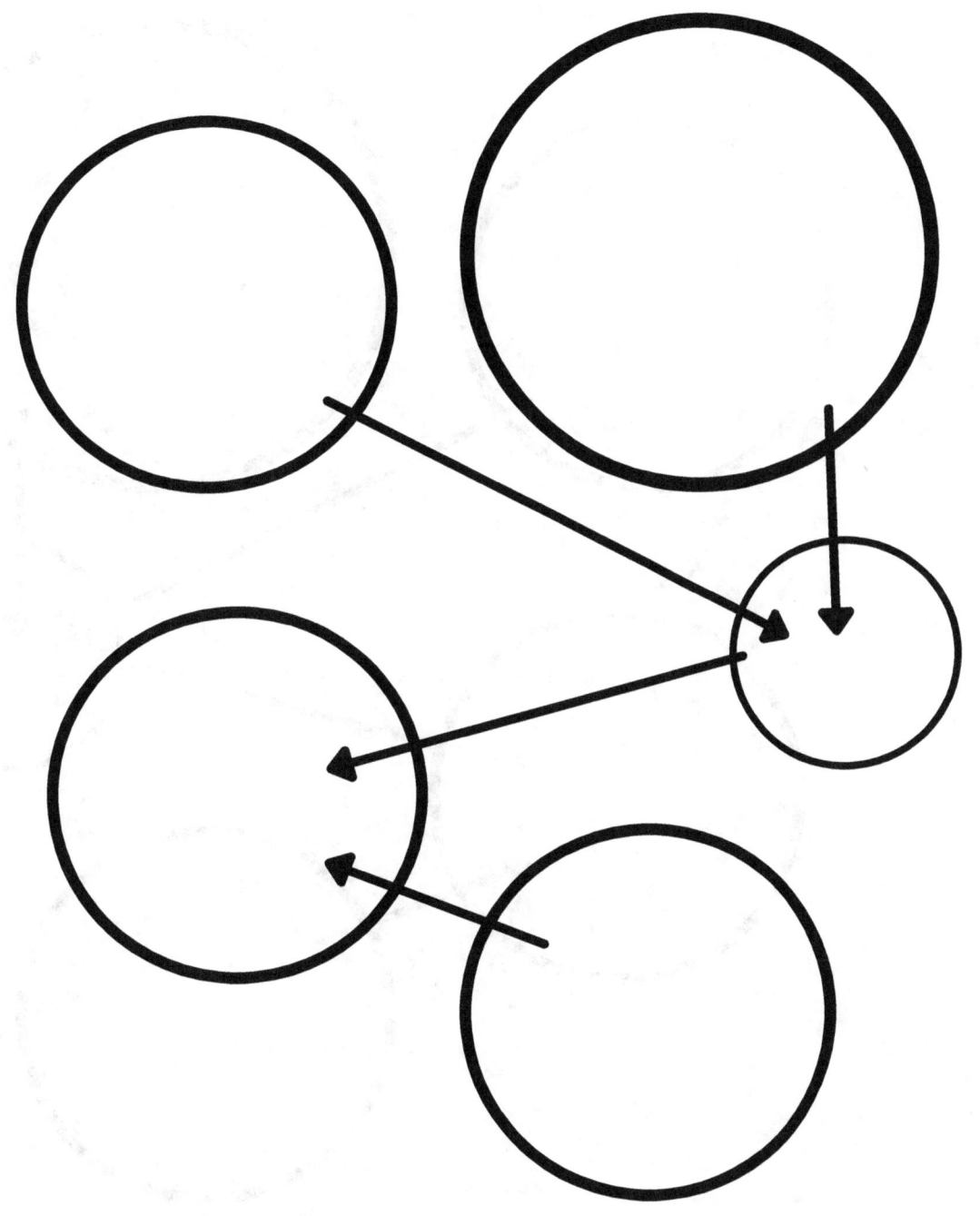

IDEAS

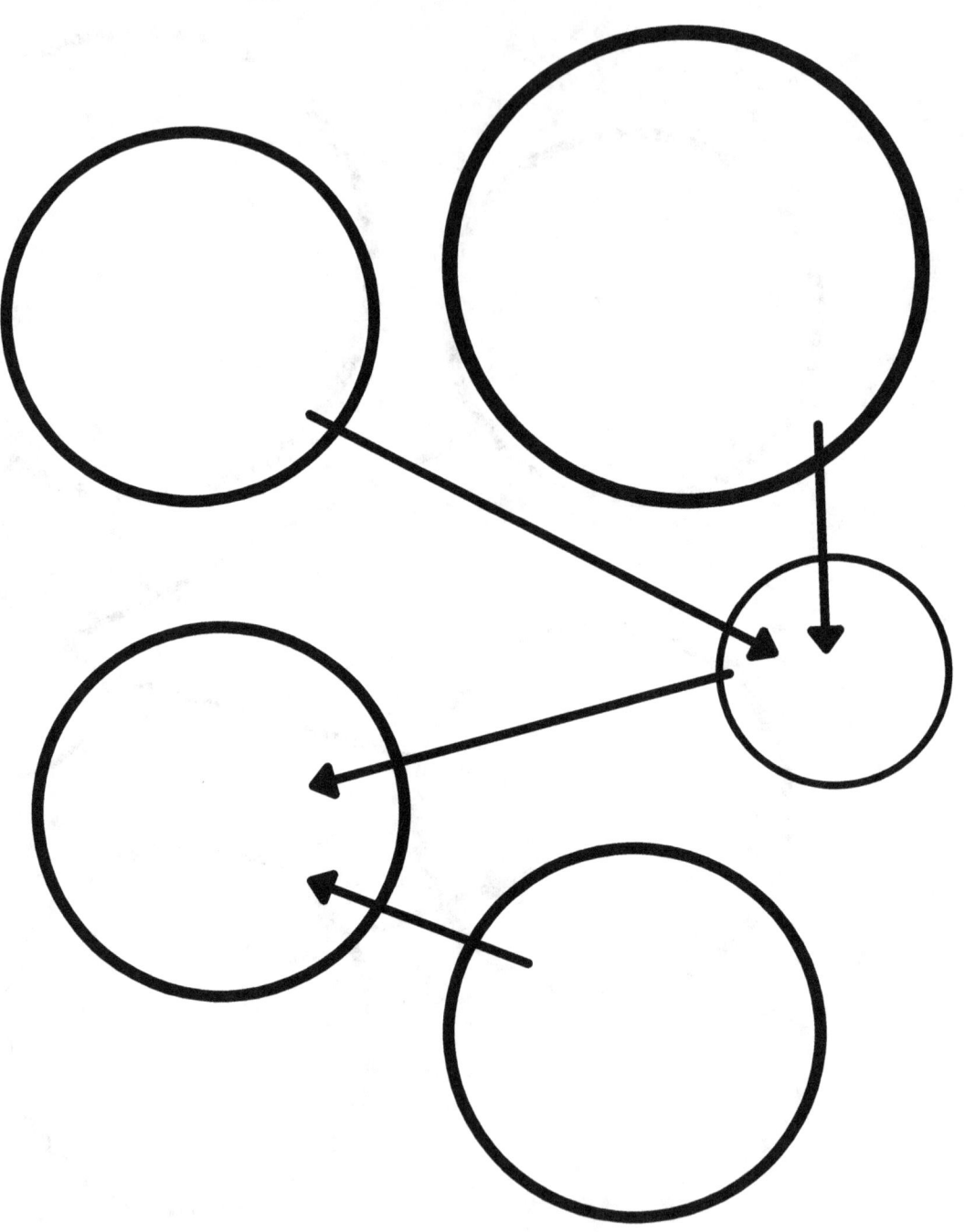

IDEAS

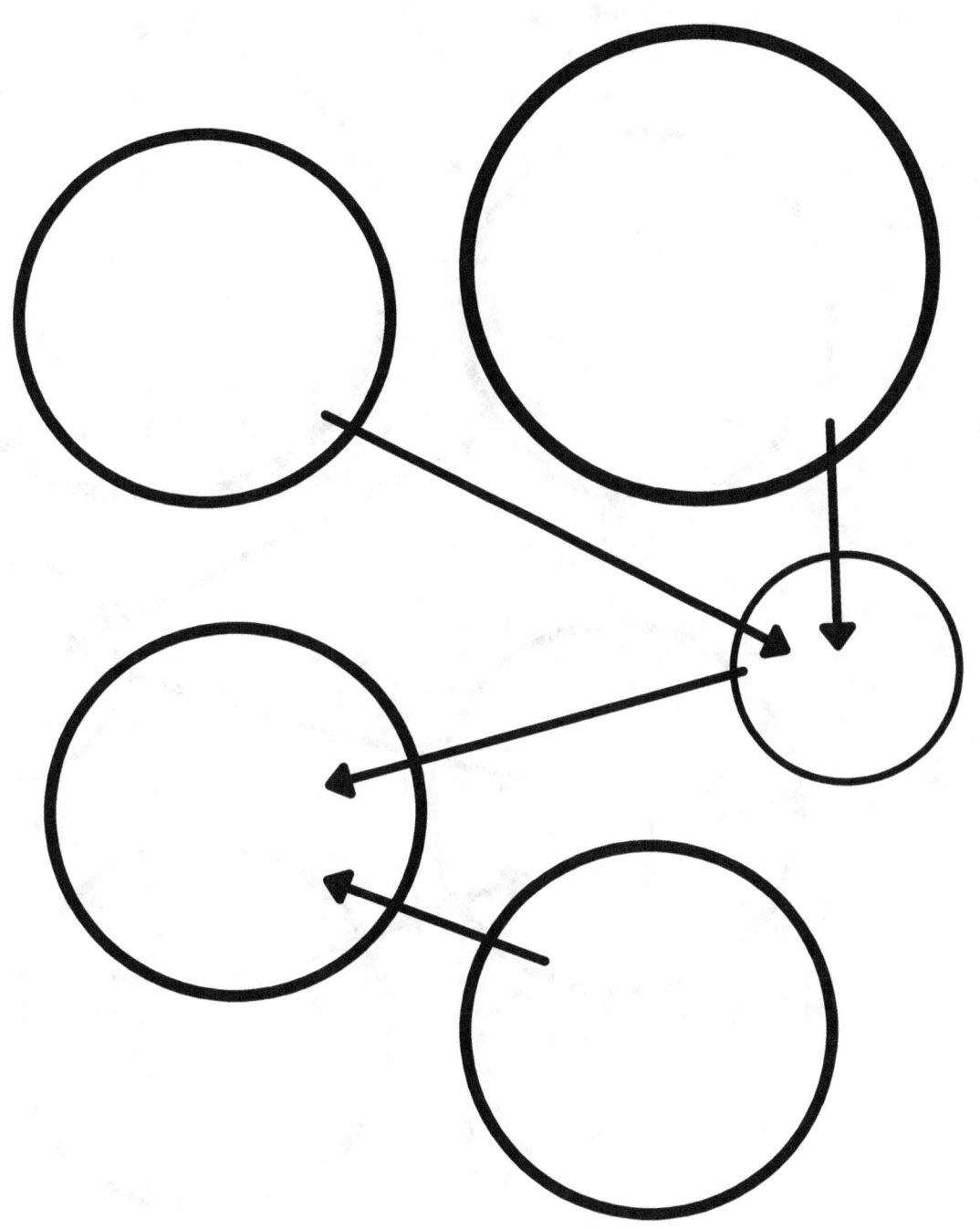

IDEAS

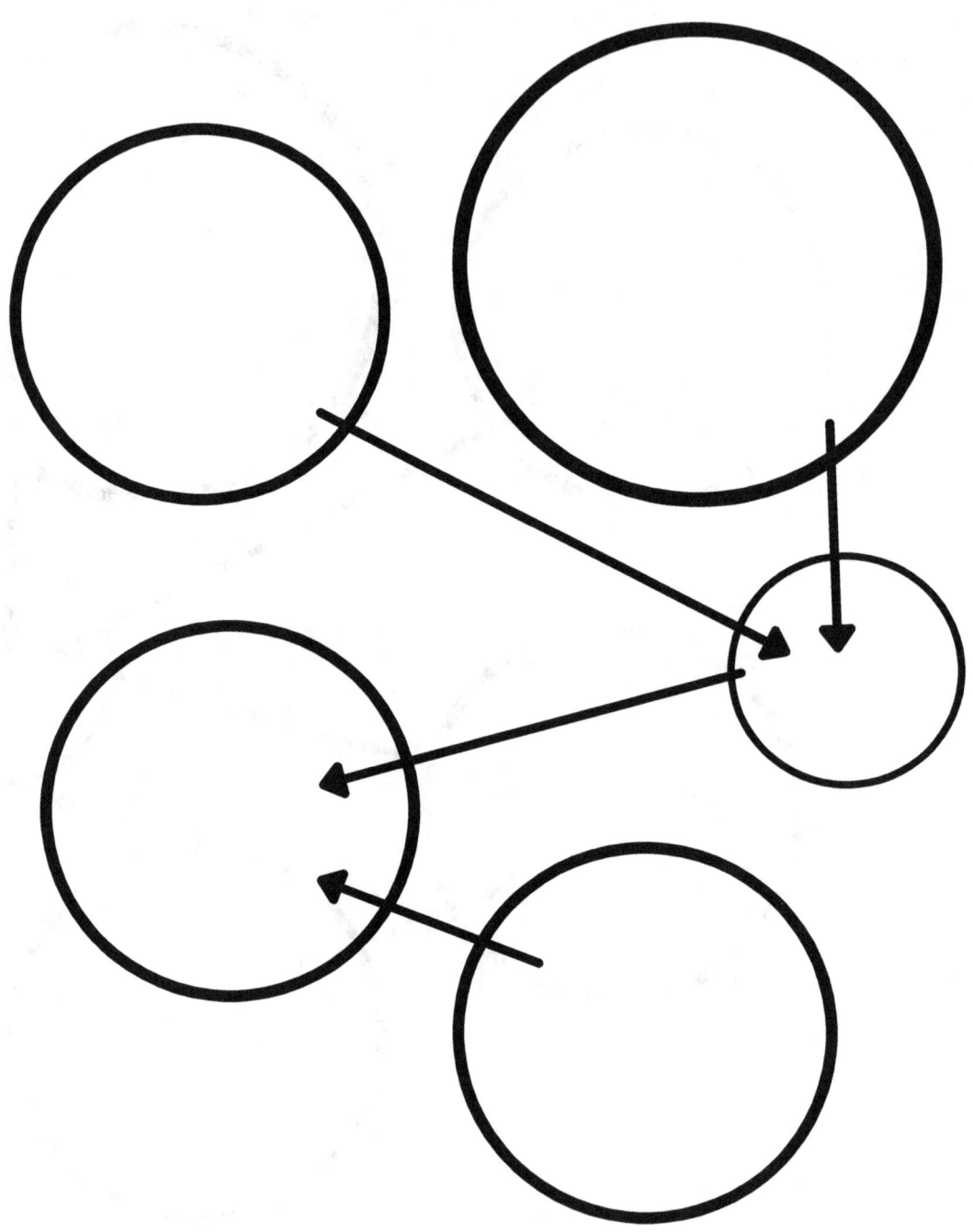

IDEAS

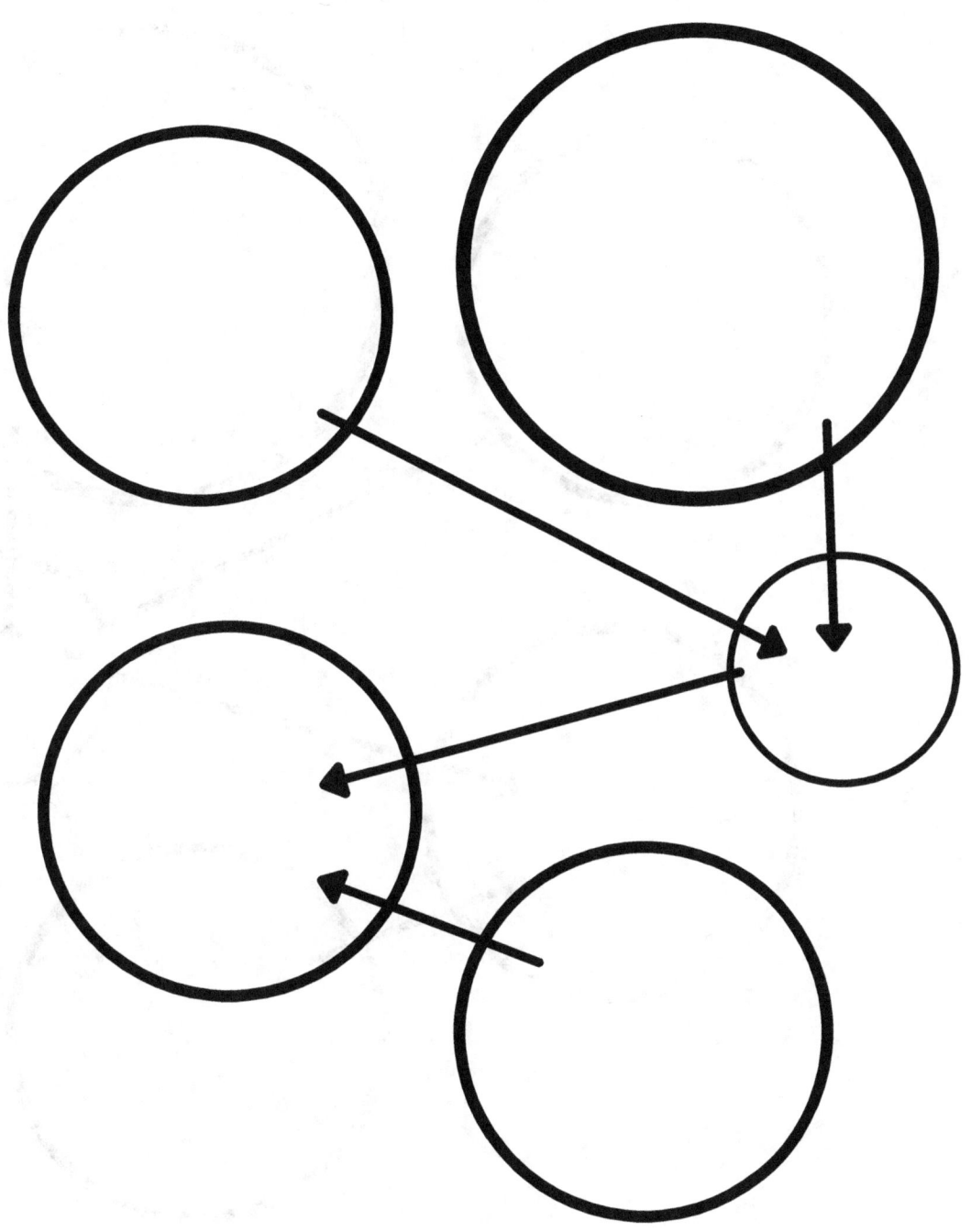

IDEAS

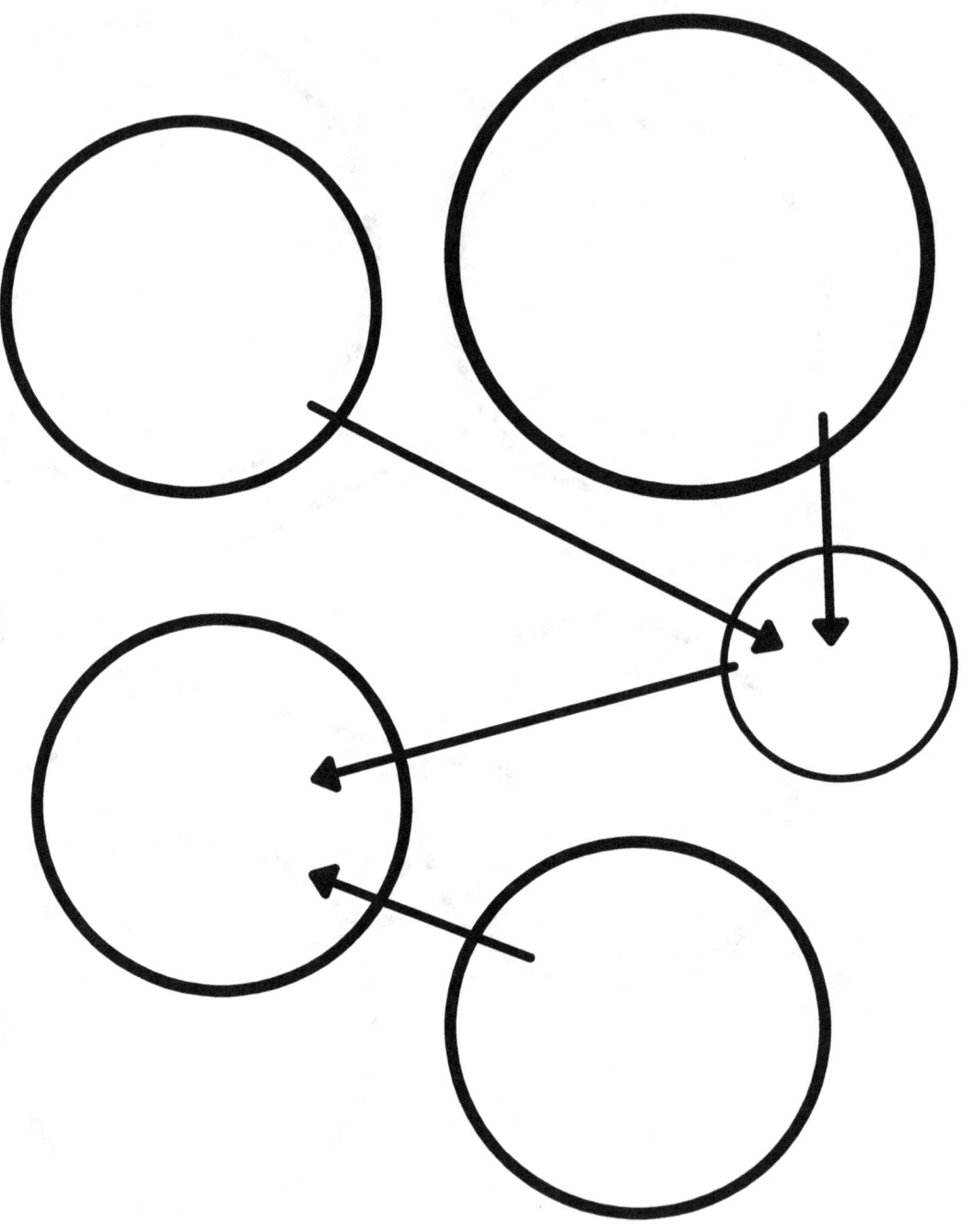

IDEAS

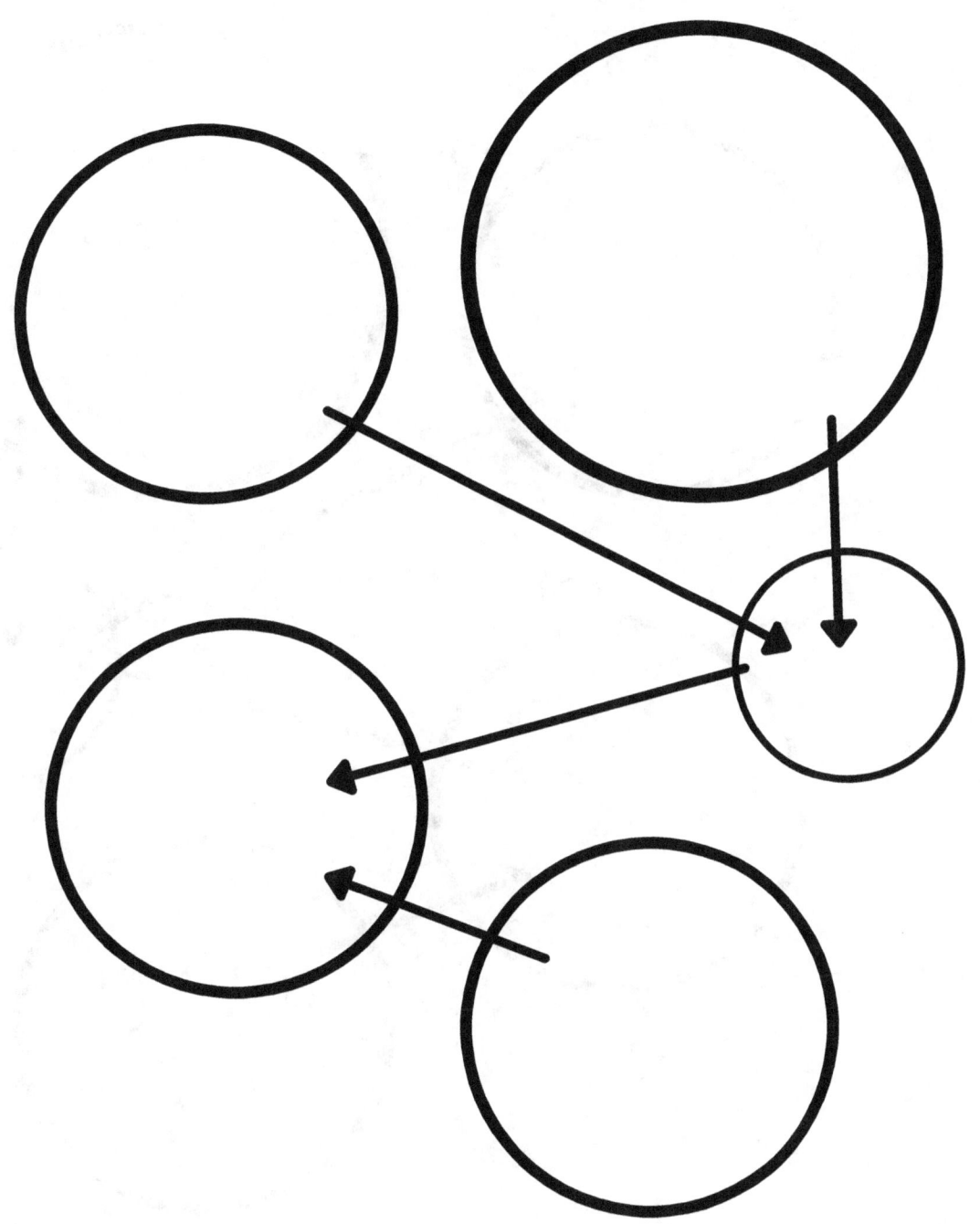

IDEAS

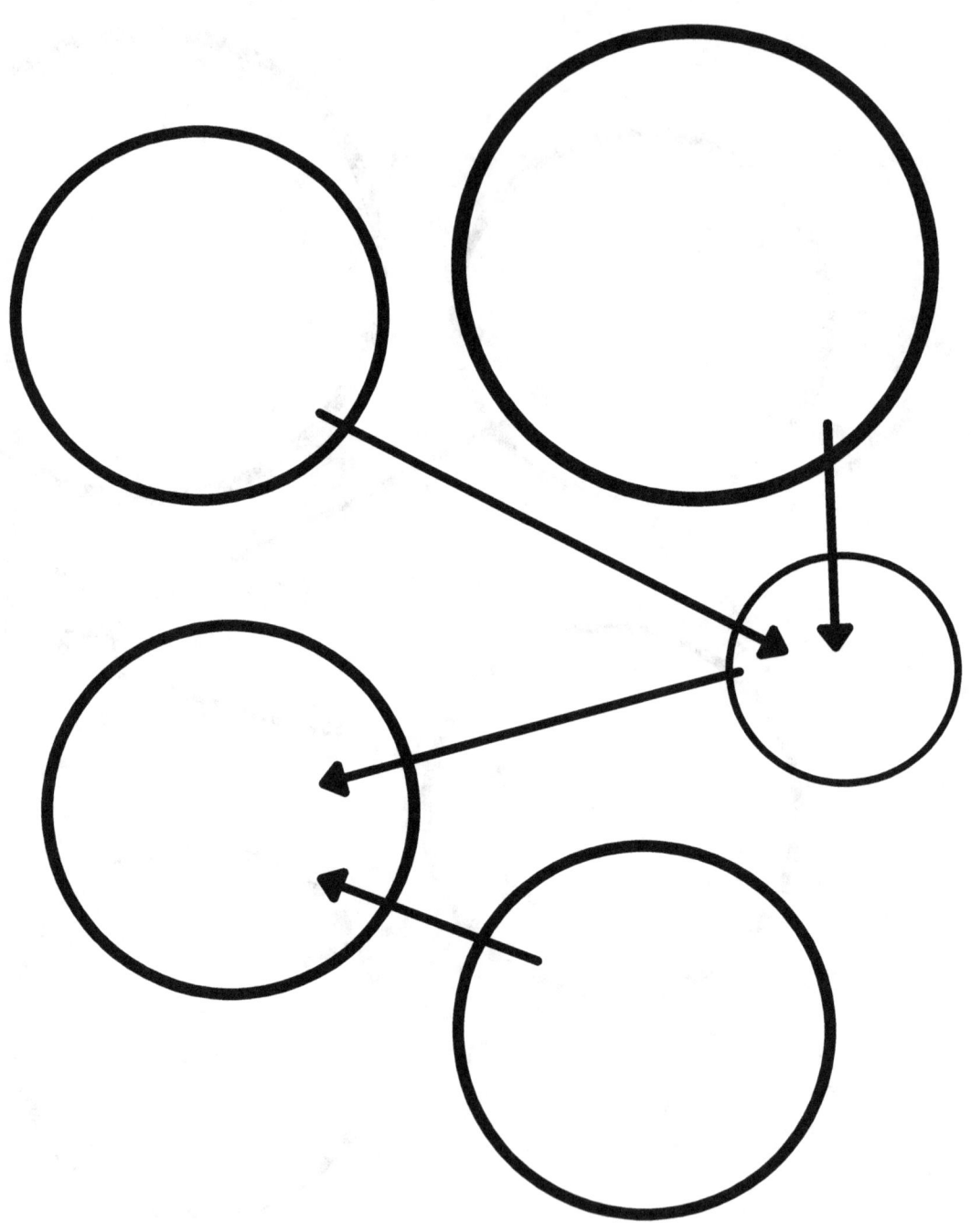

IDEAS

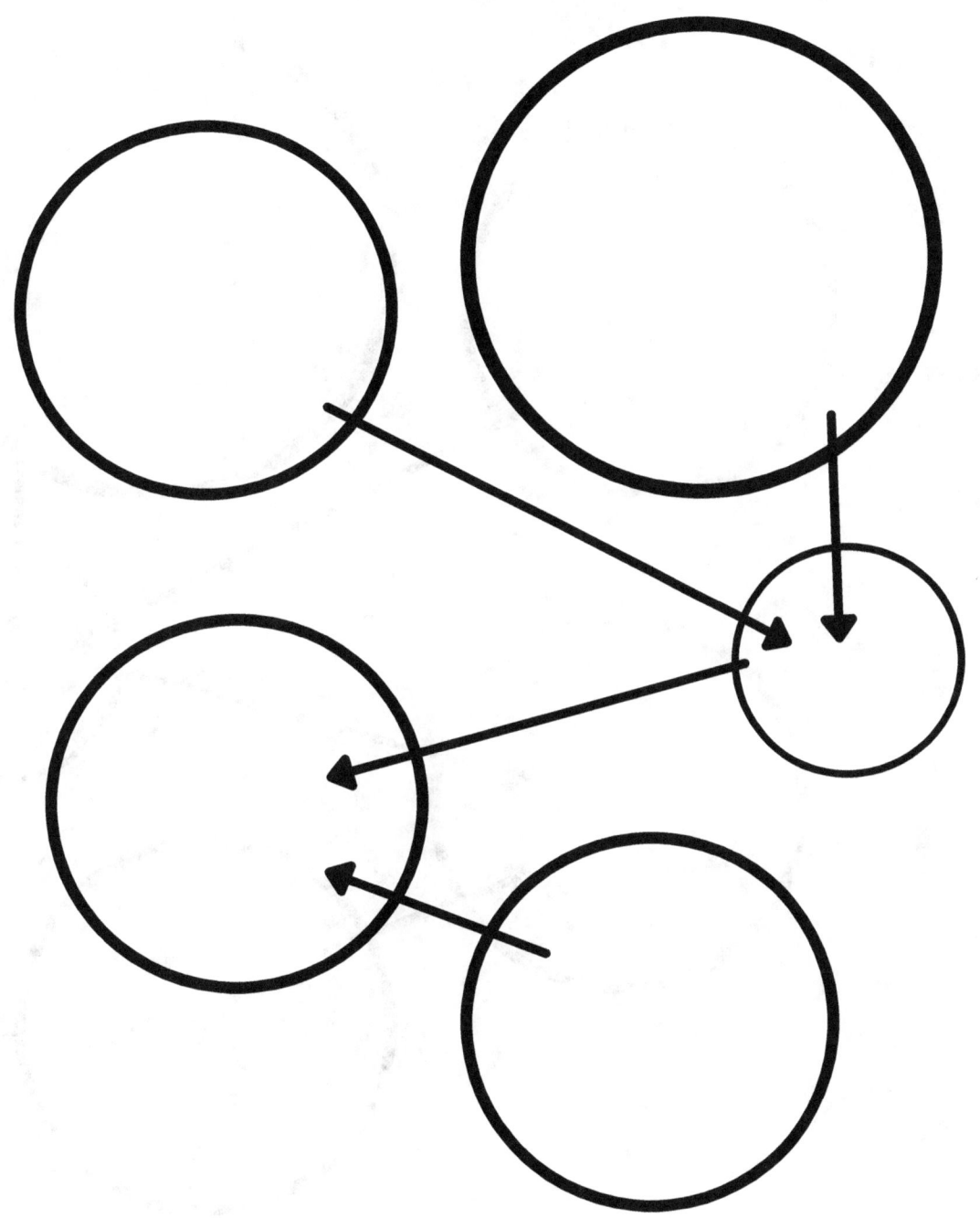

IDEAS

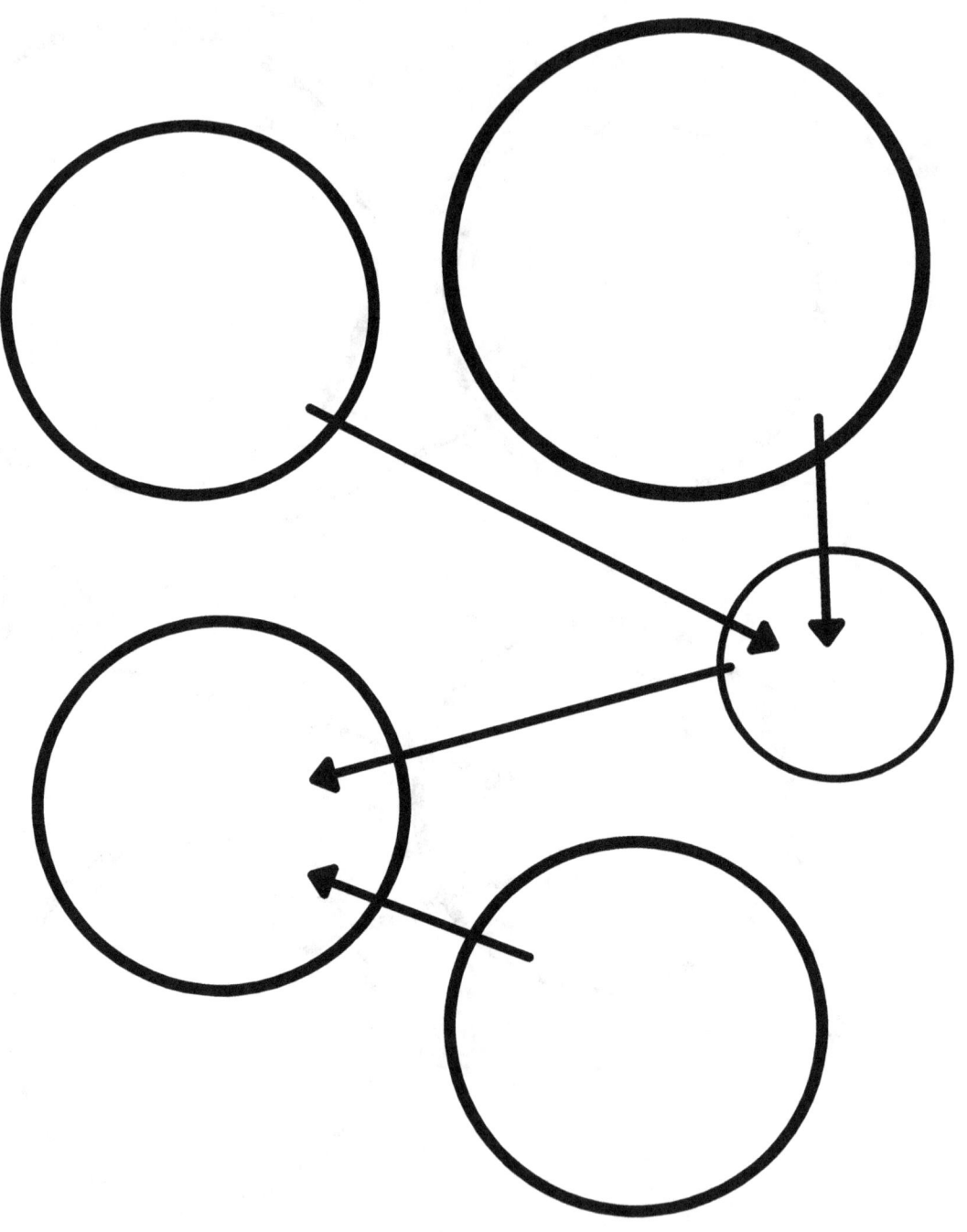

IDEAS

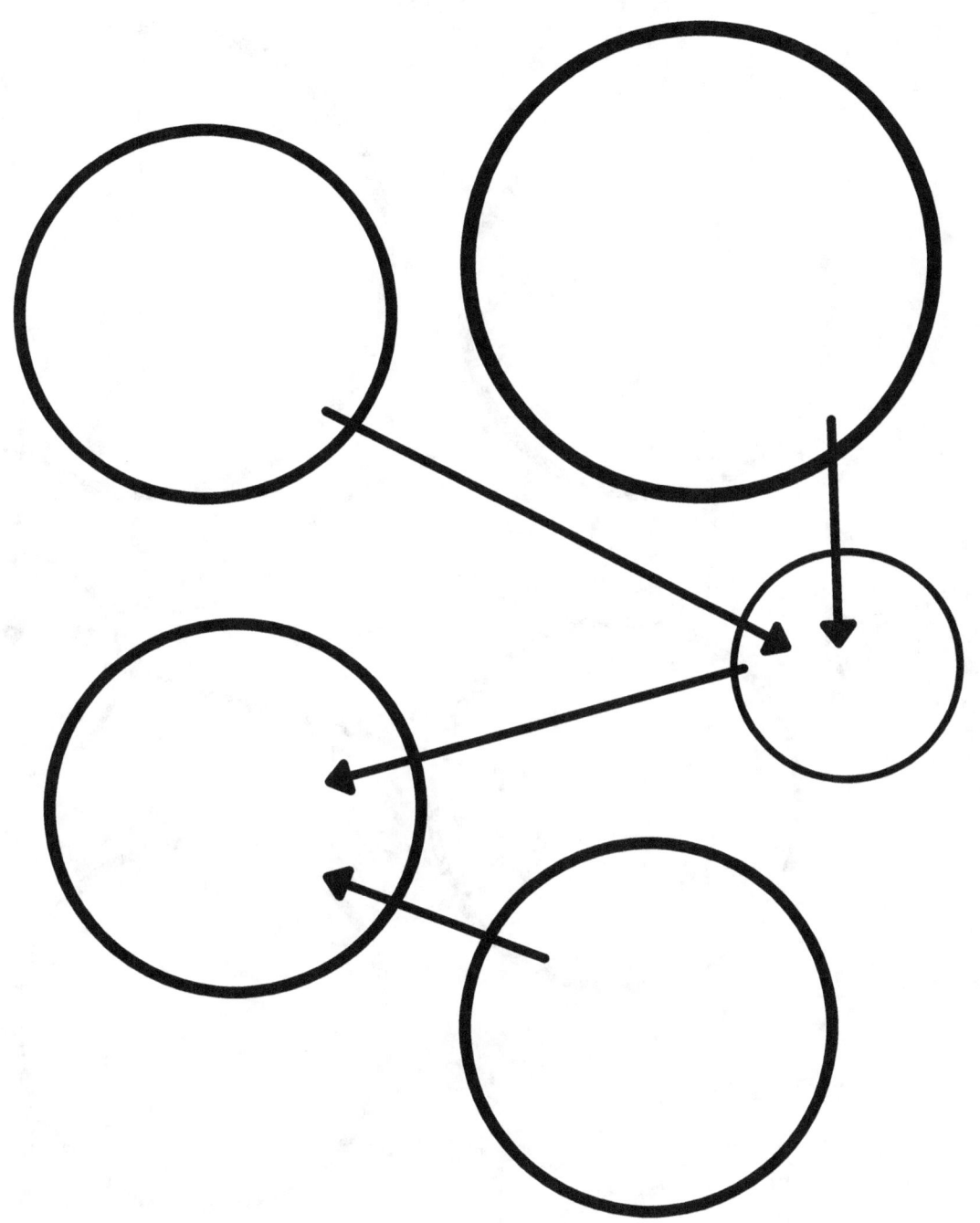

IDEAS

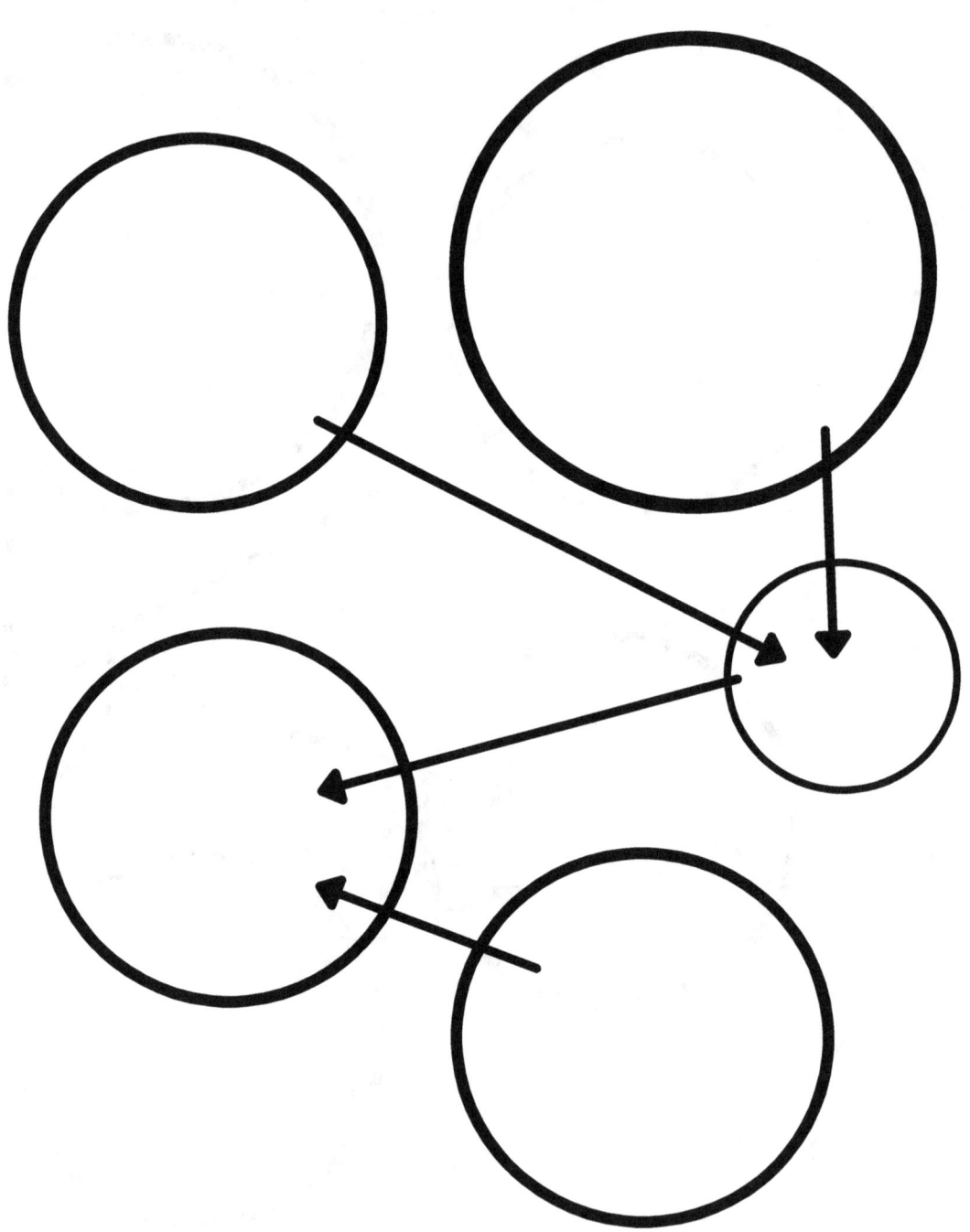

IDEAS

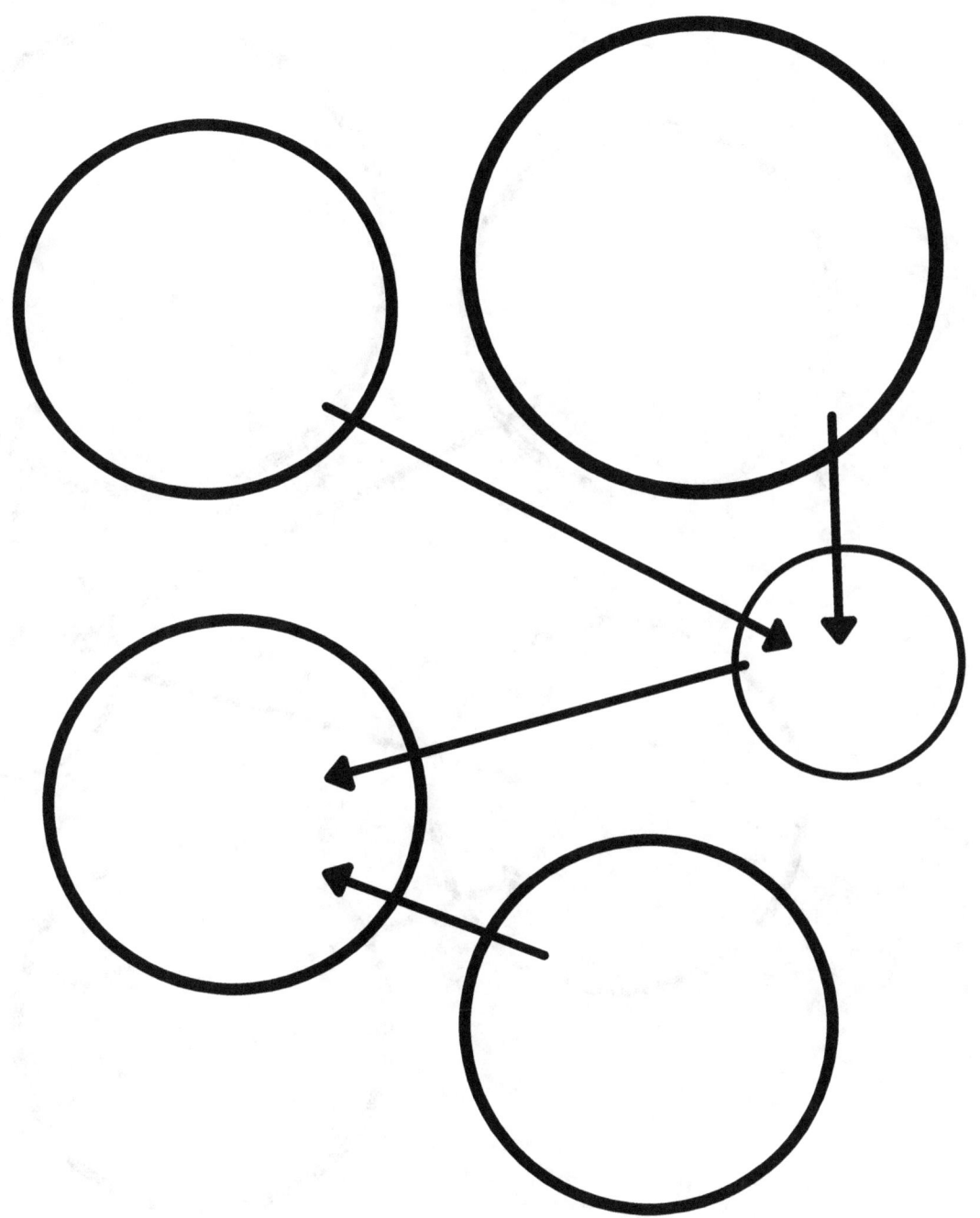

IDEAS

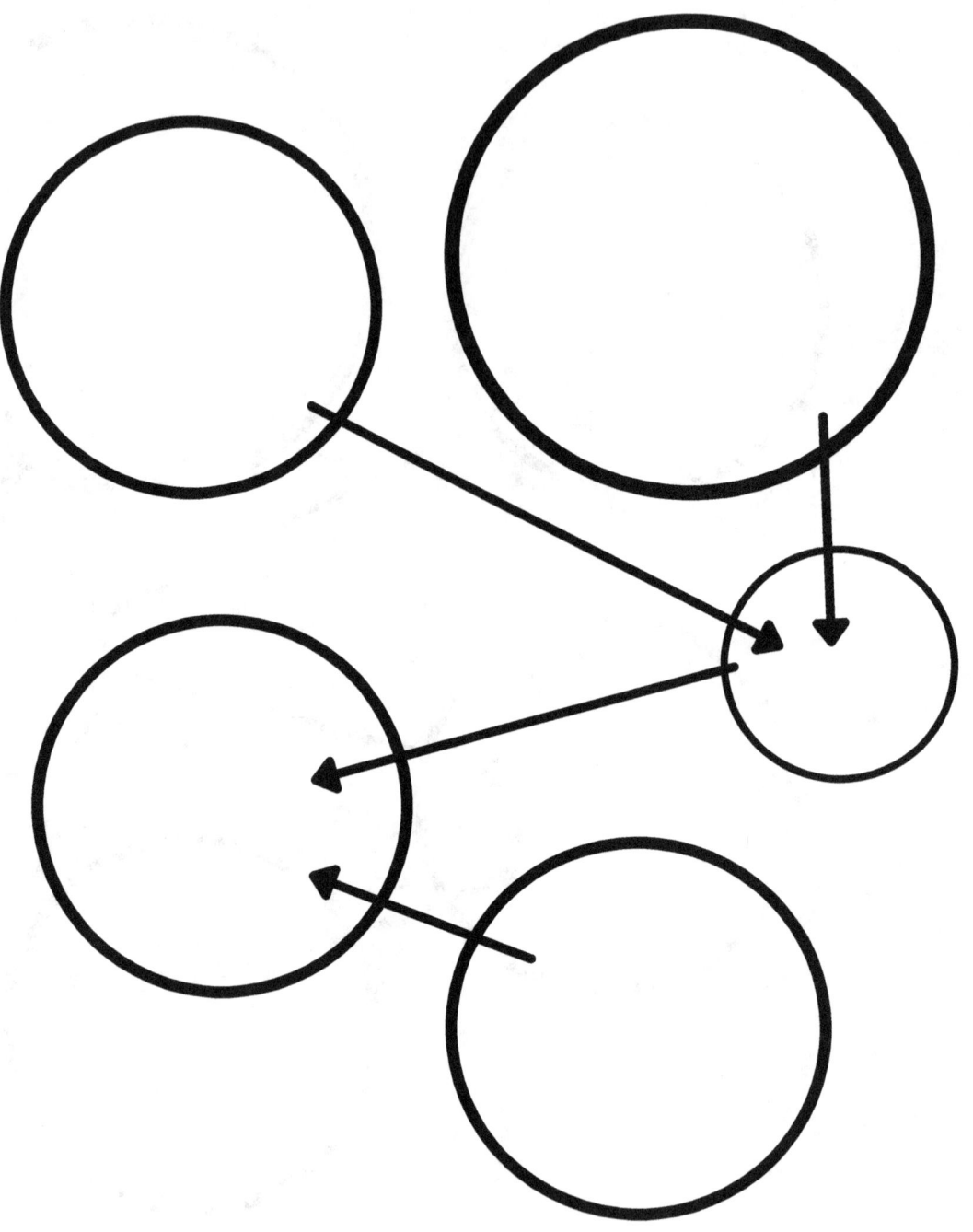

IDEAS

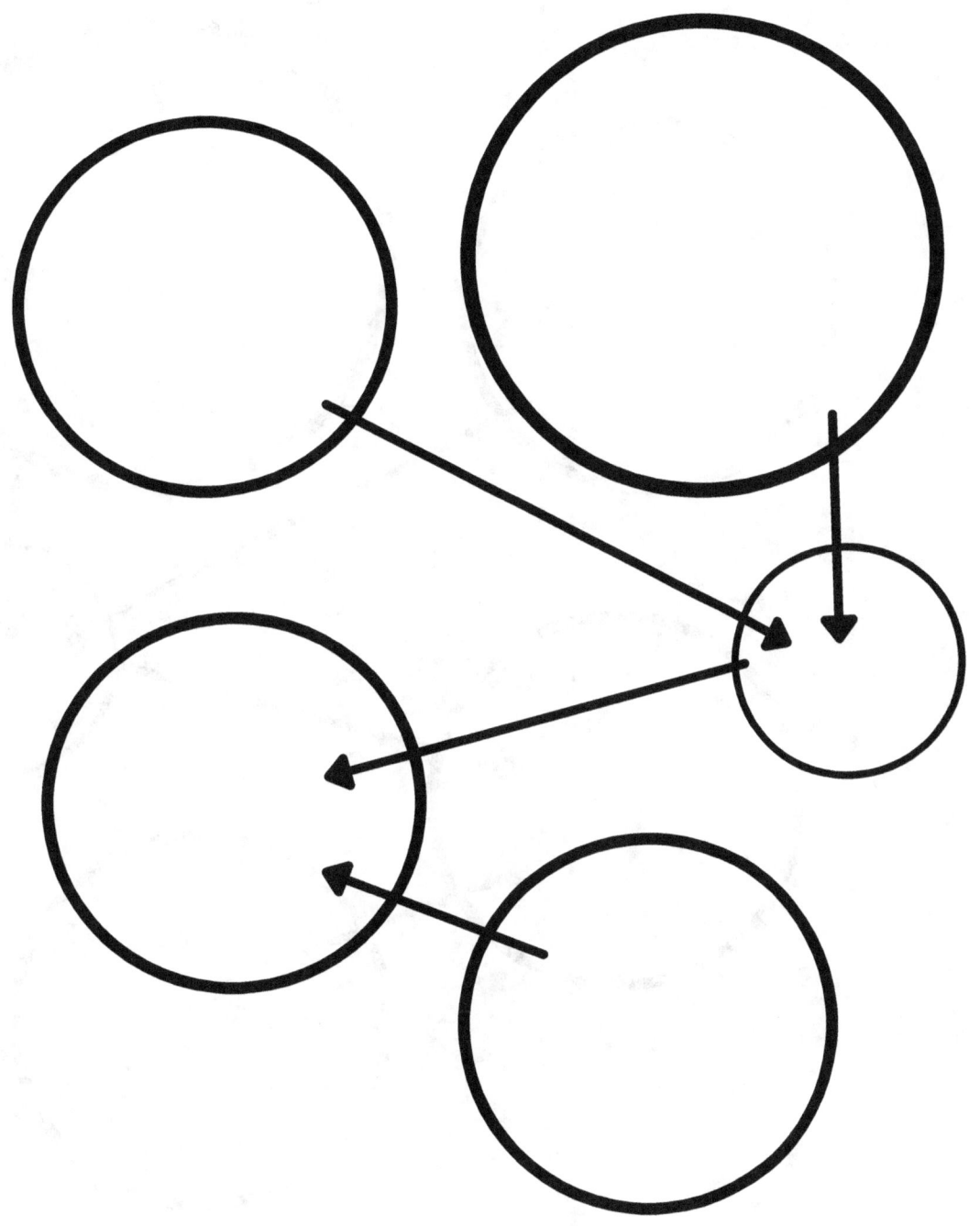

IDEAS

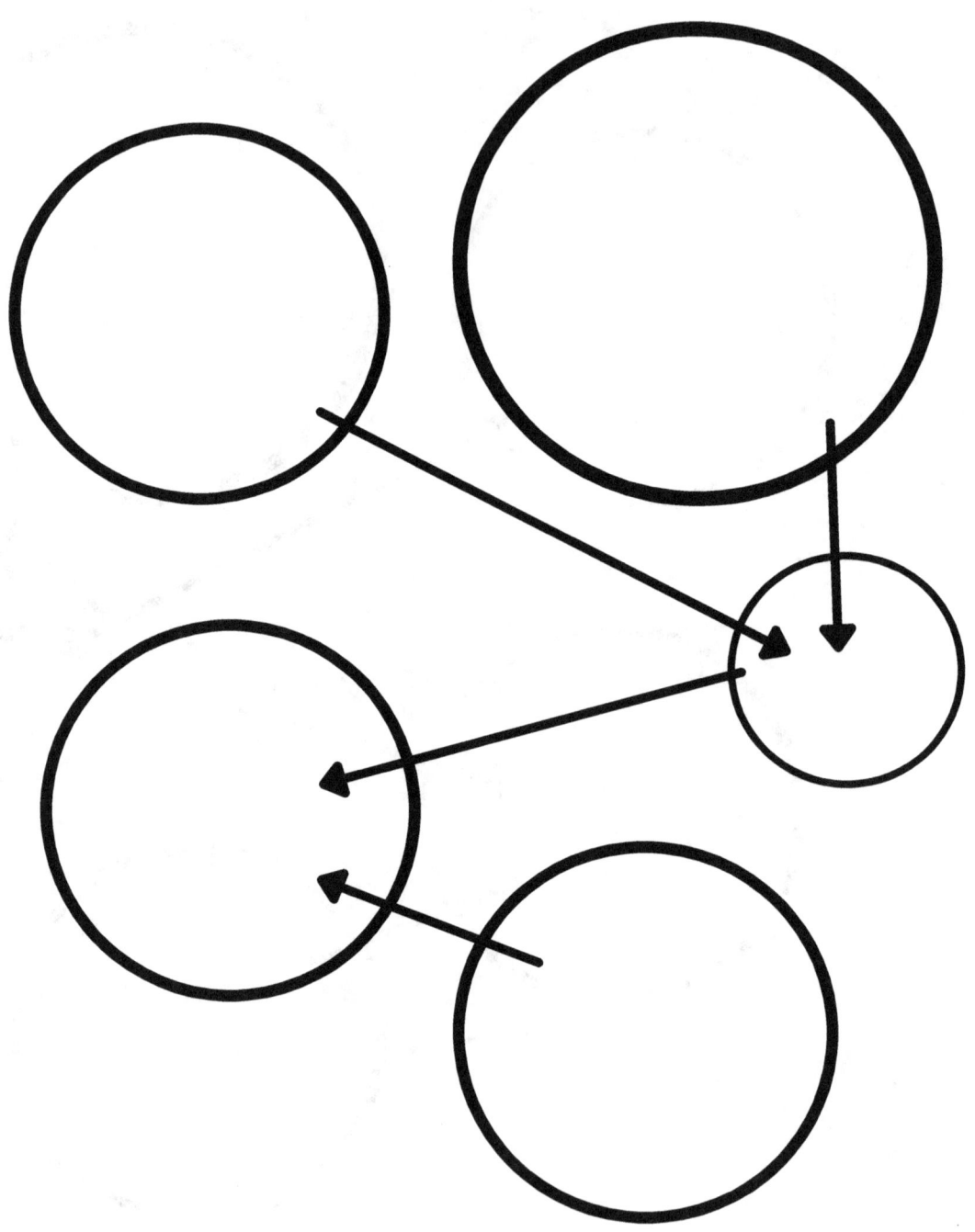

IDEAS

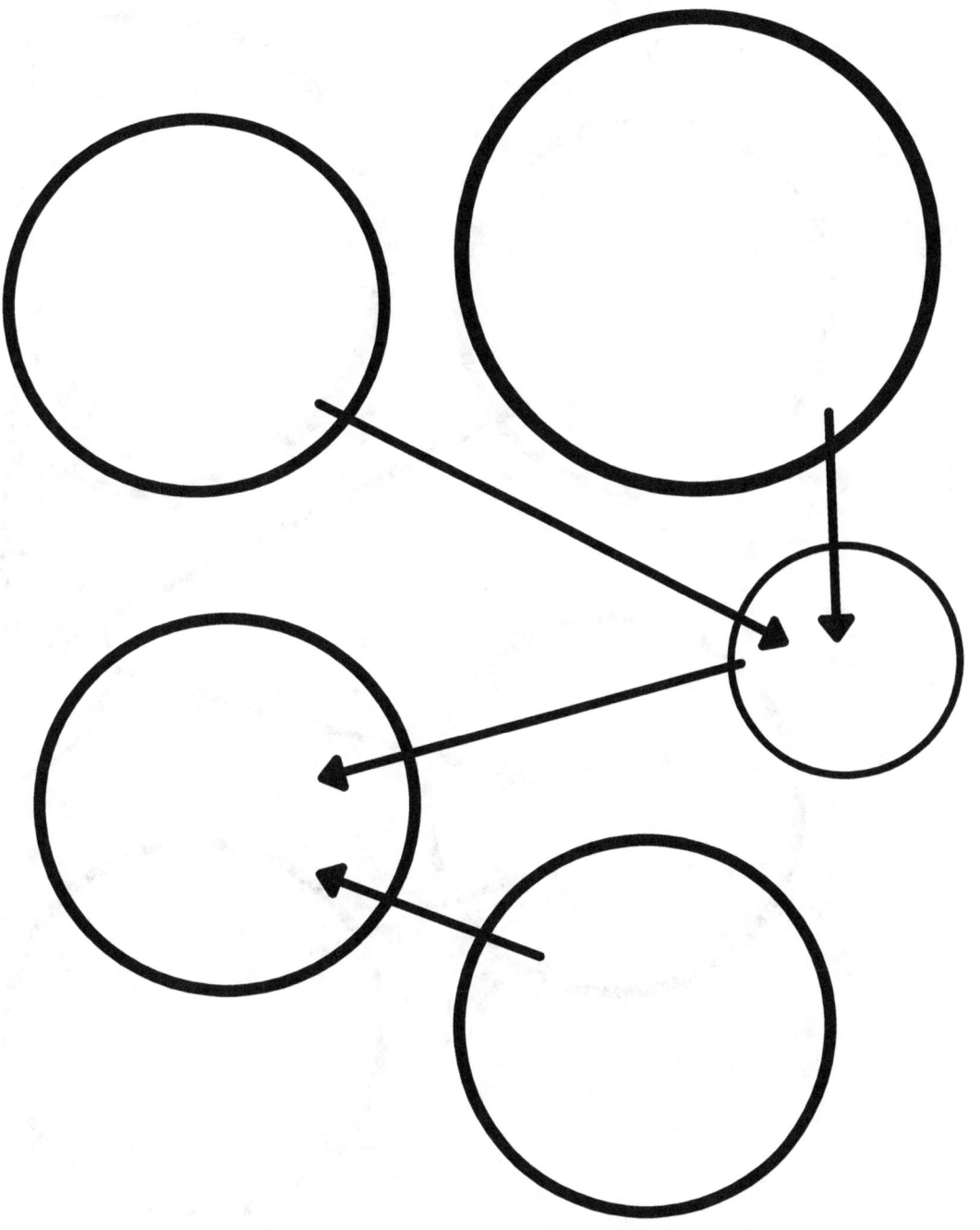

IDEAS

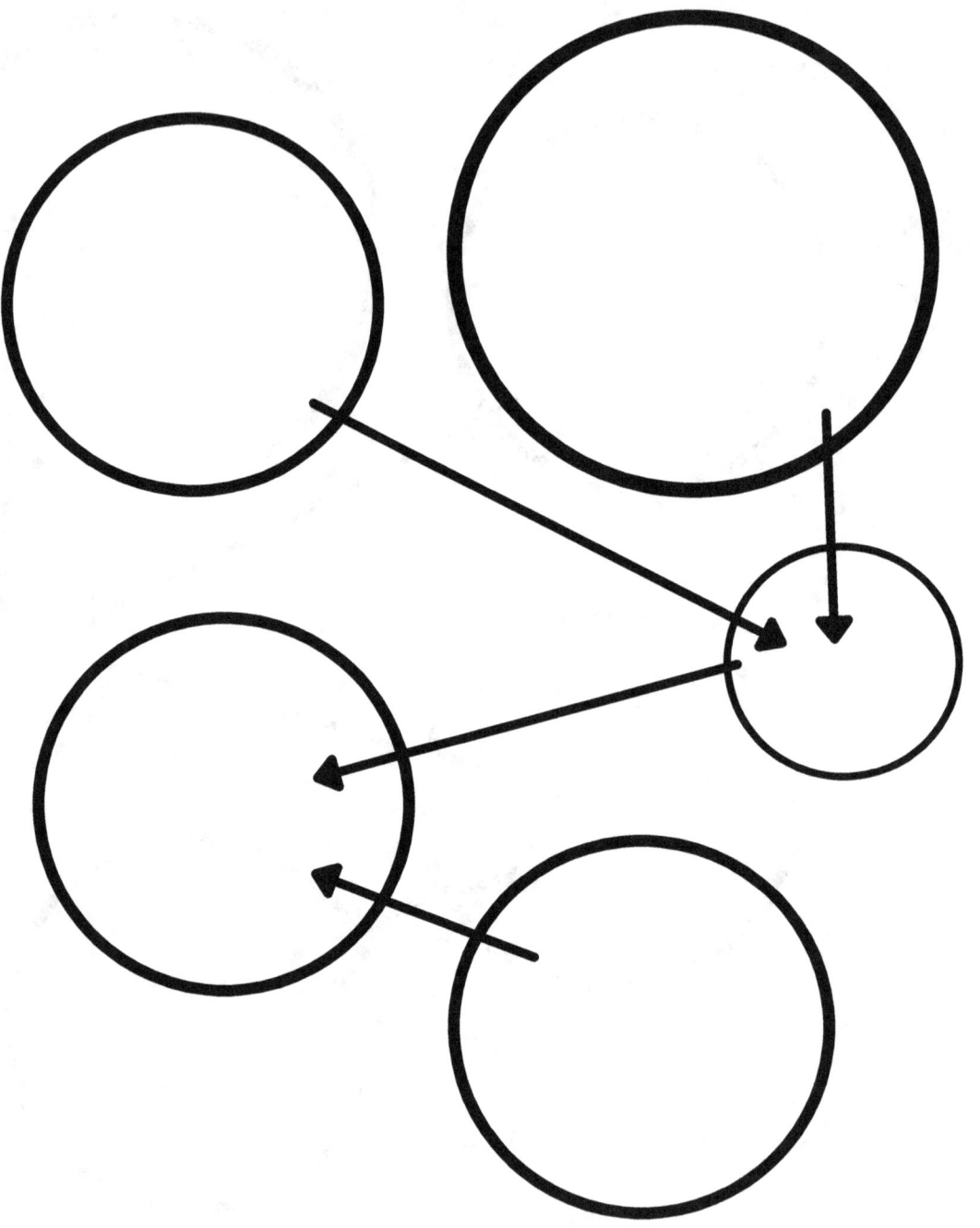

IDEAS

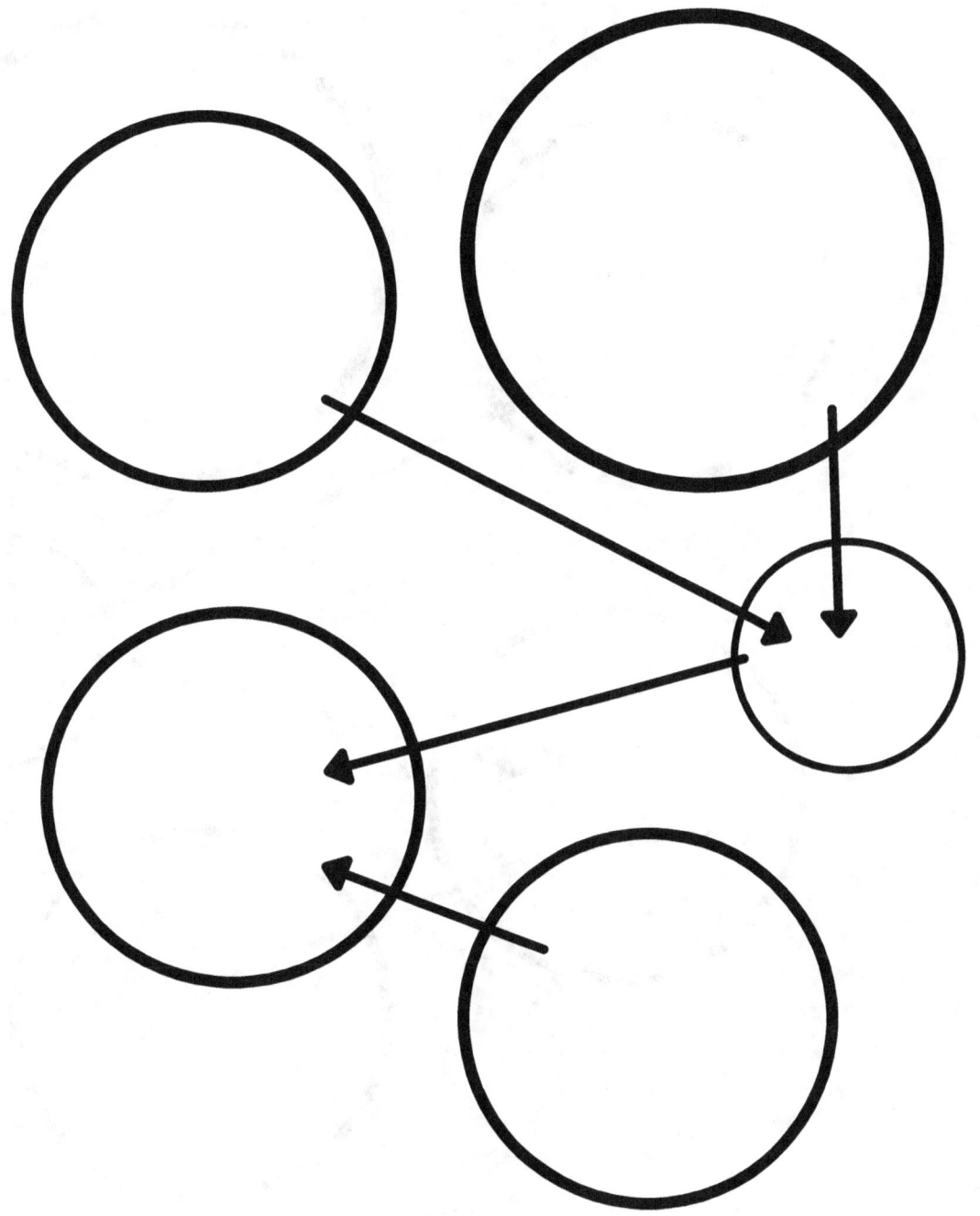

IDEAS

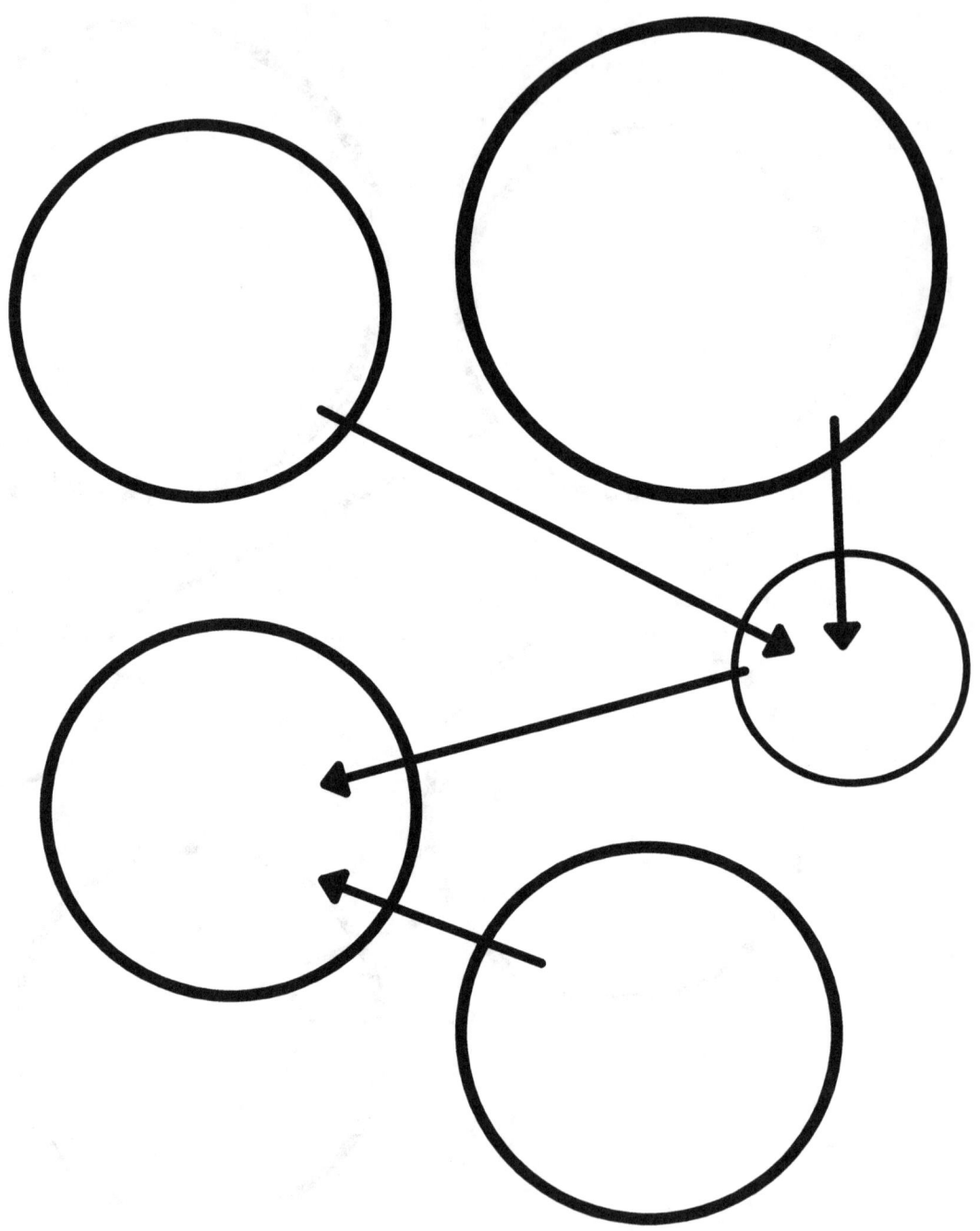

IDEAS

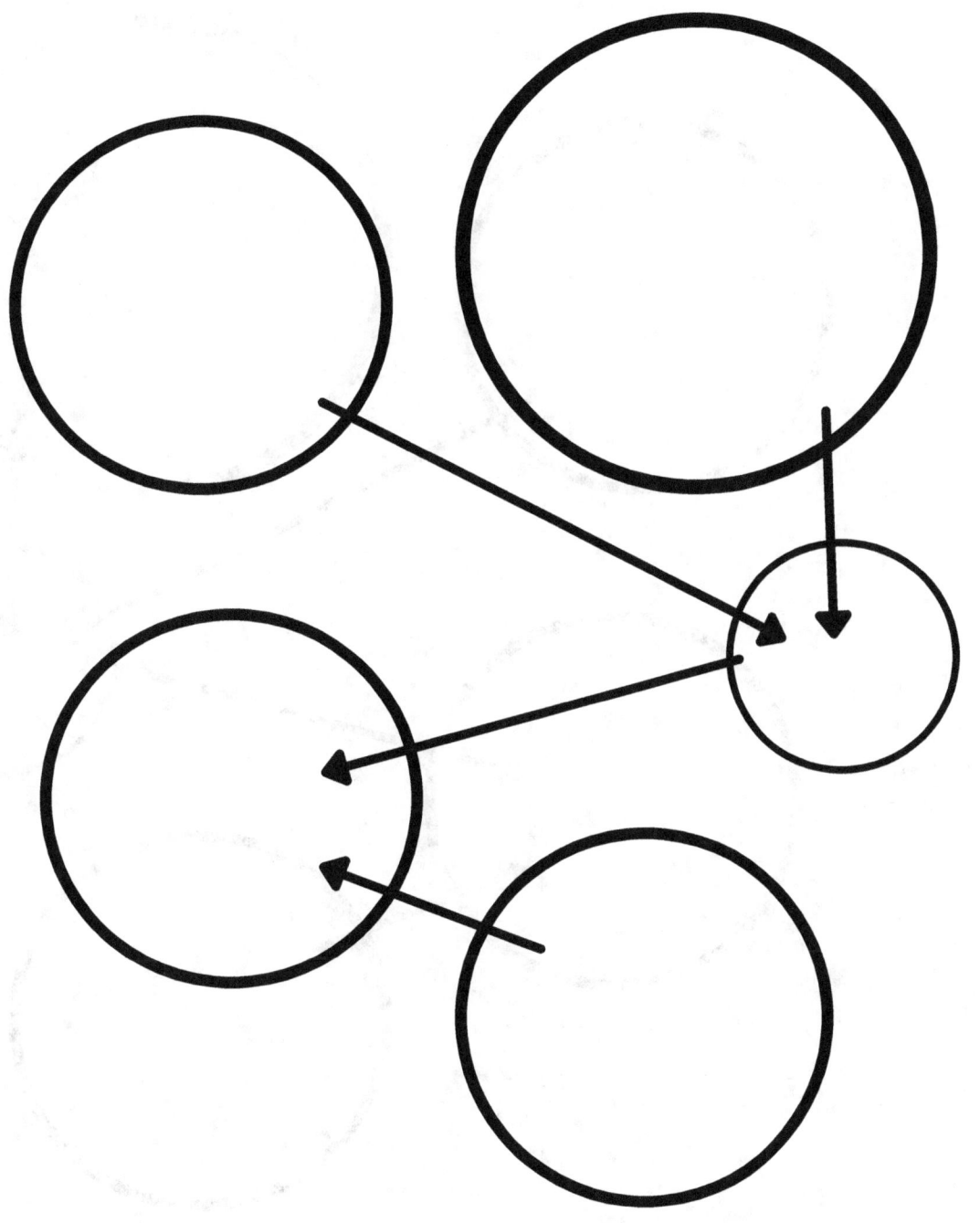

IDEAS

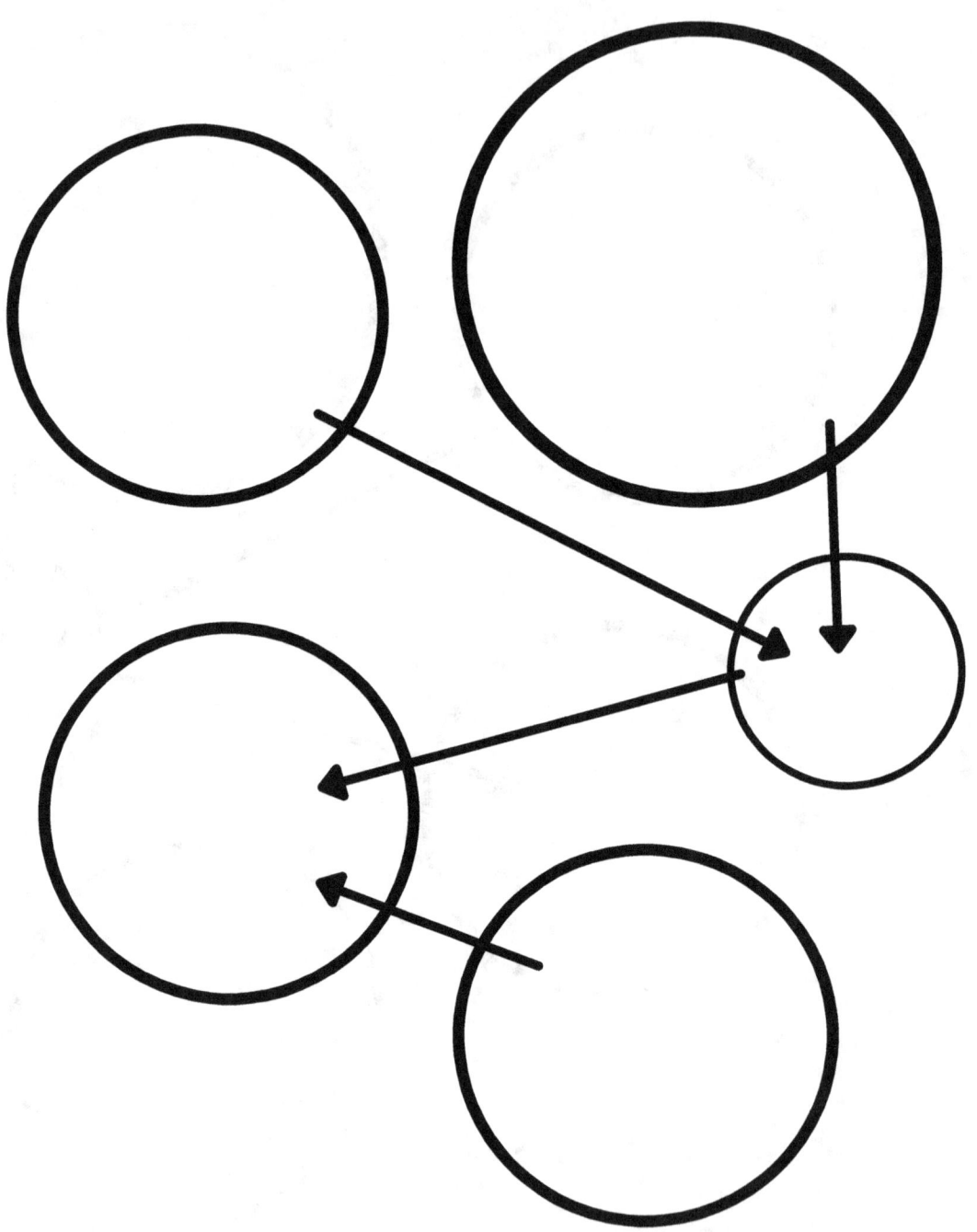

IDEAS

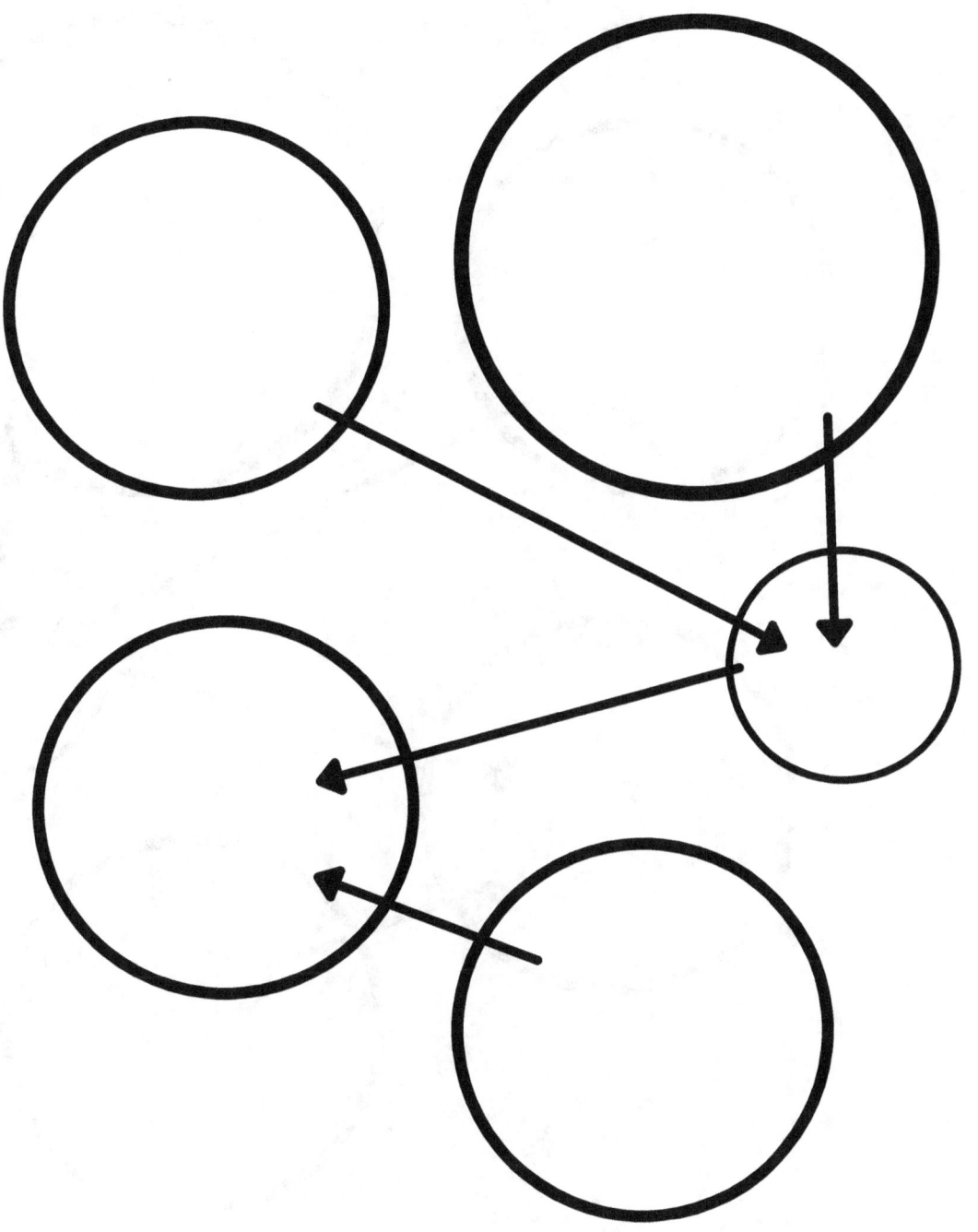

IDEAS

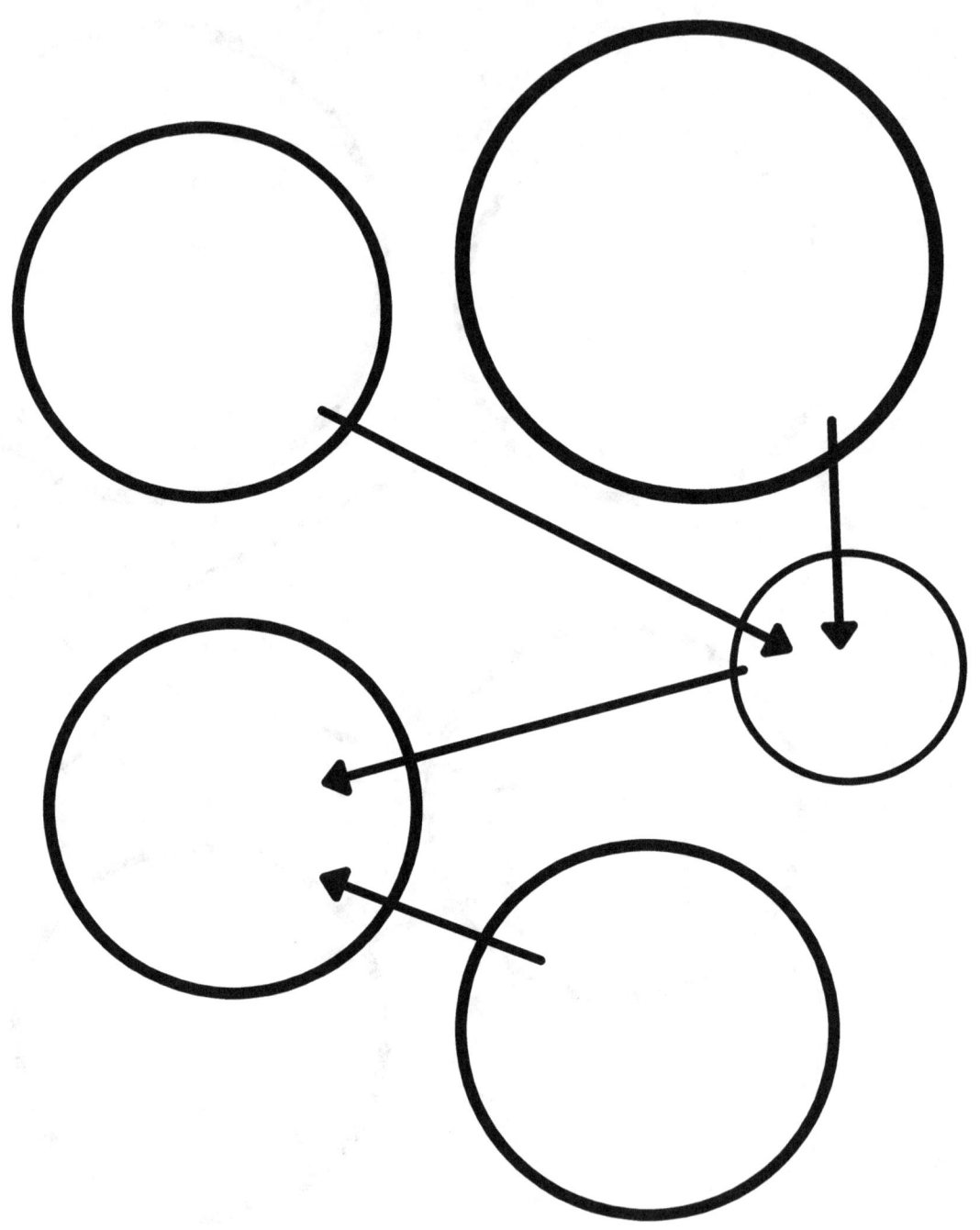

IDEAS

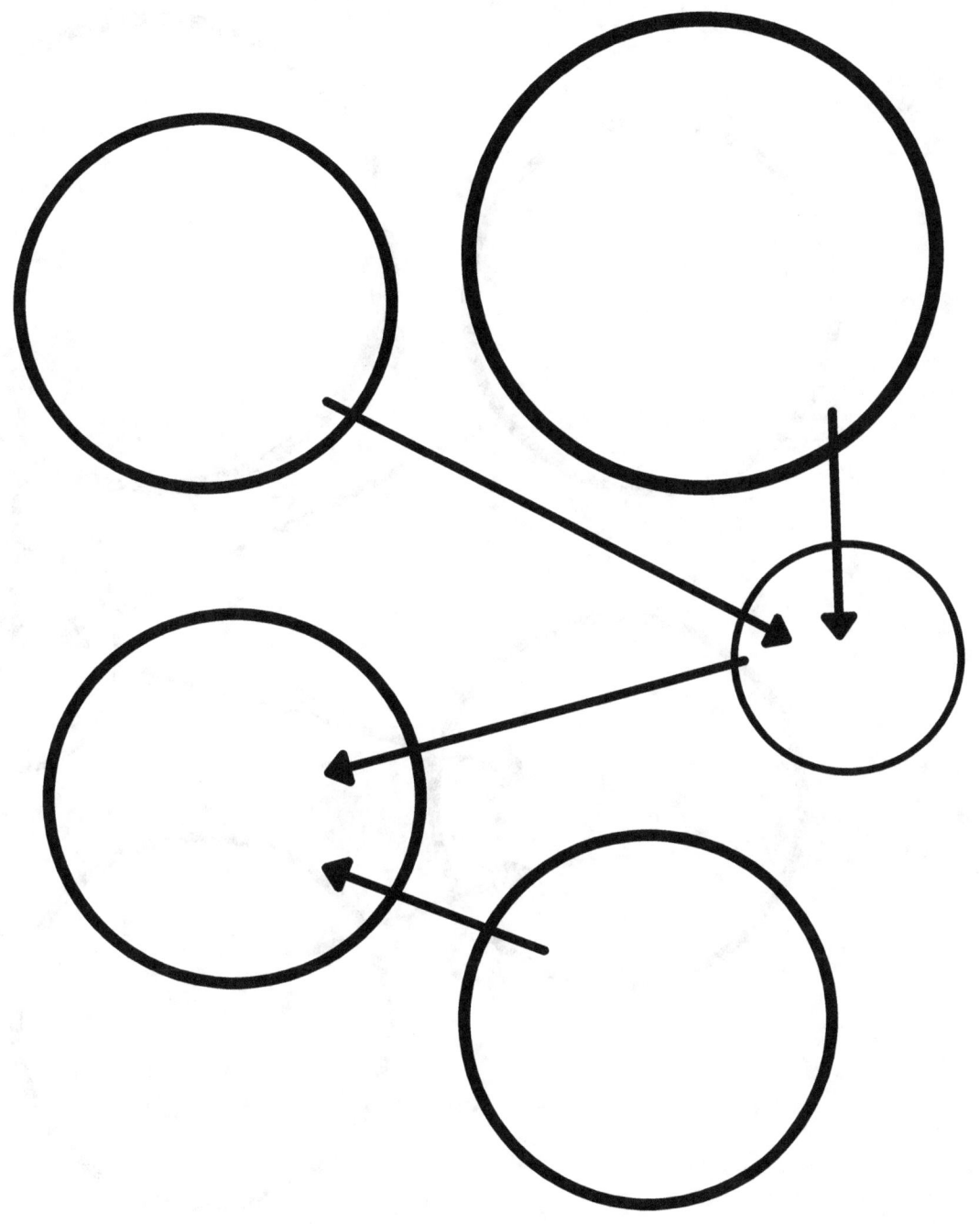

IDEAS

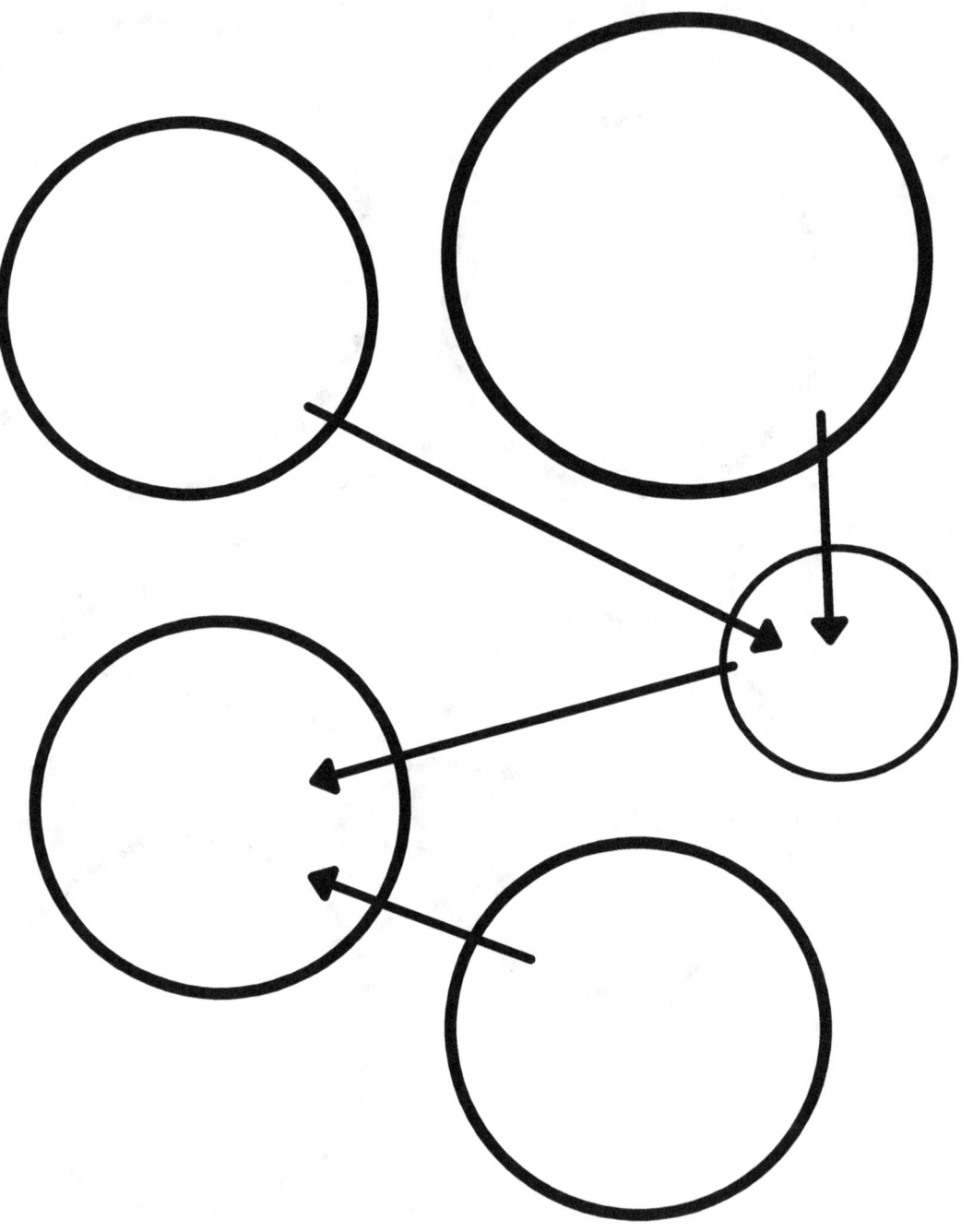

IDEAS

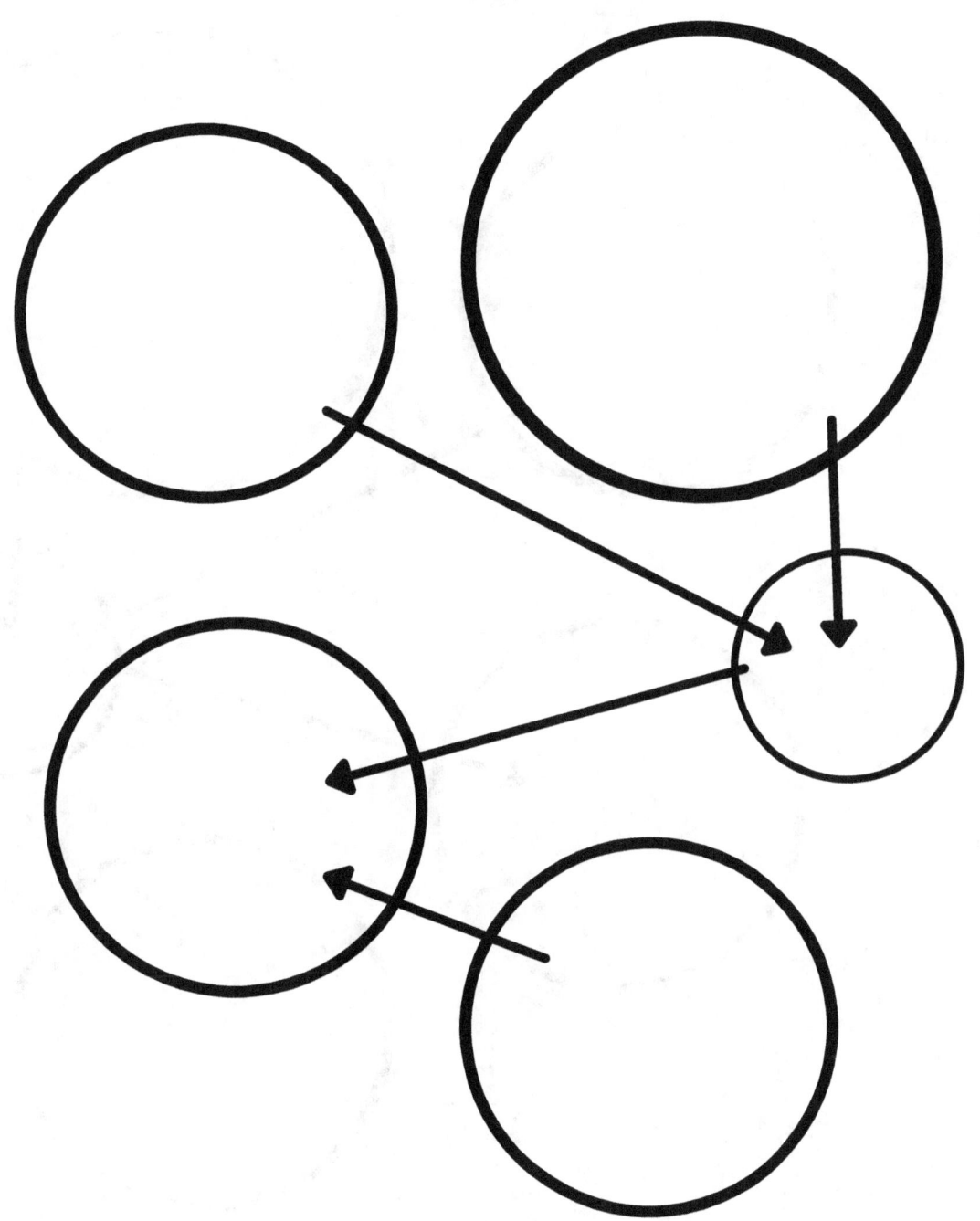

IDEAS

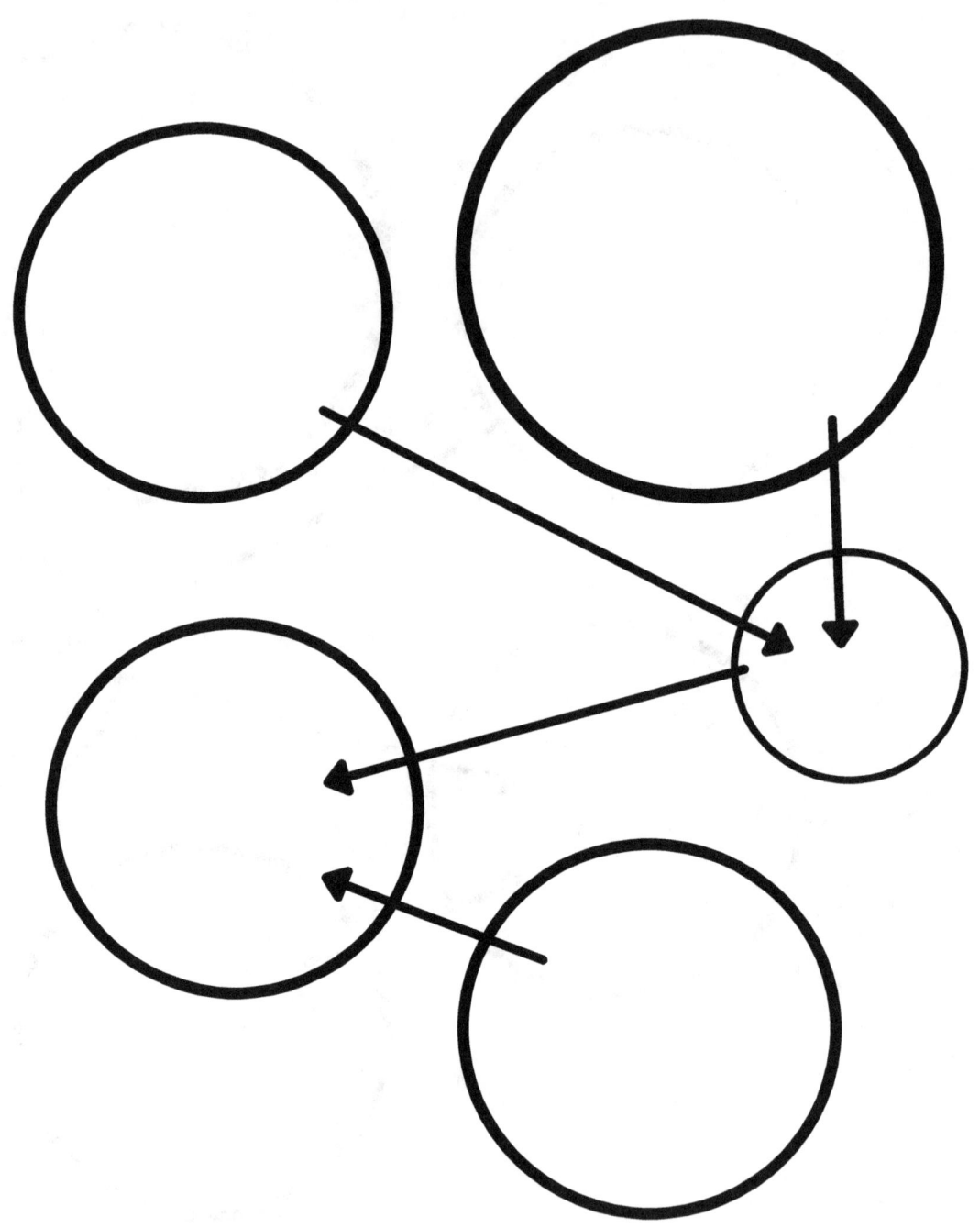

IDEAS

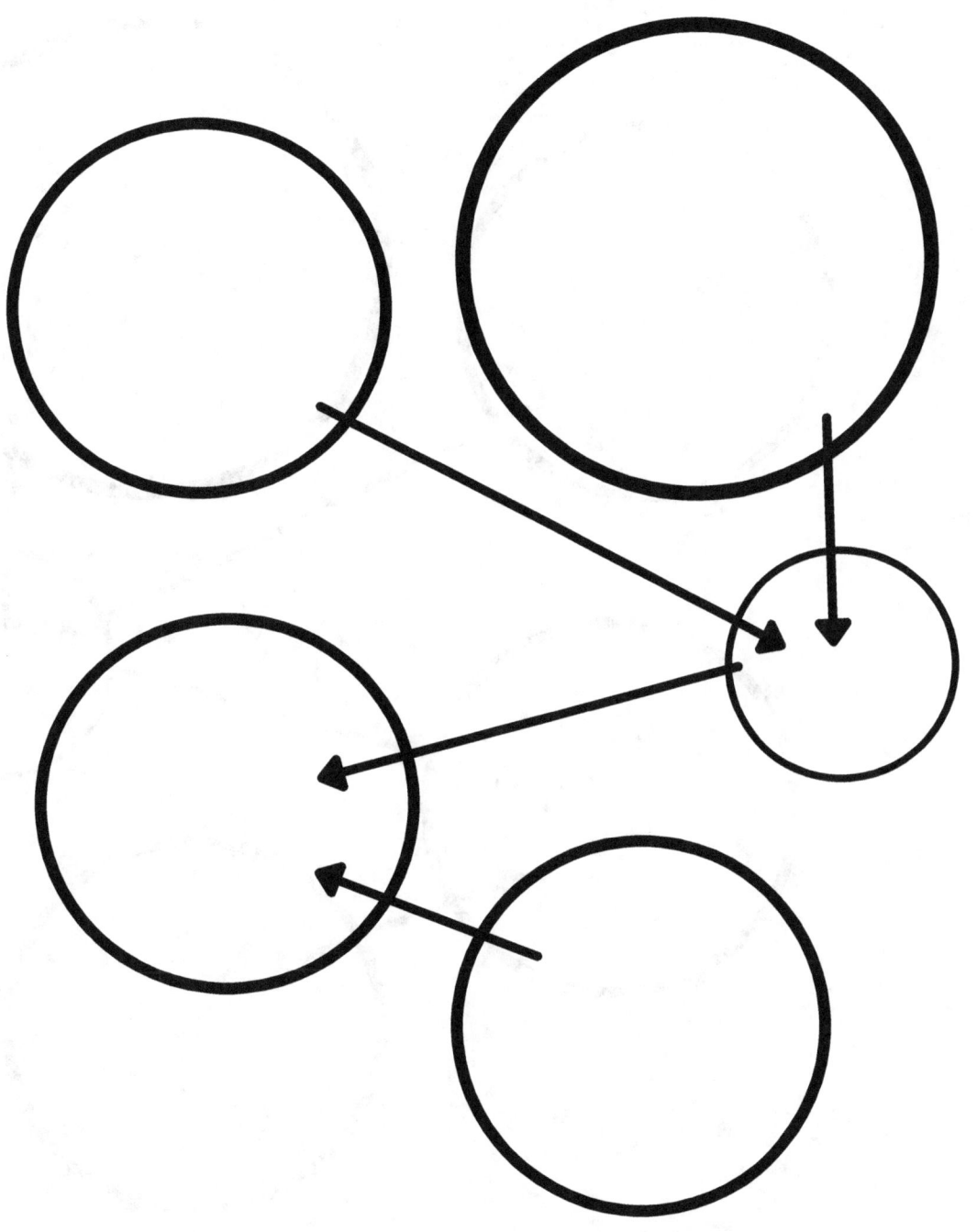

IDEAS

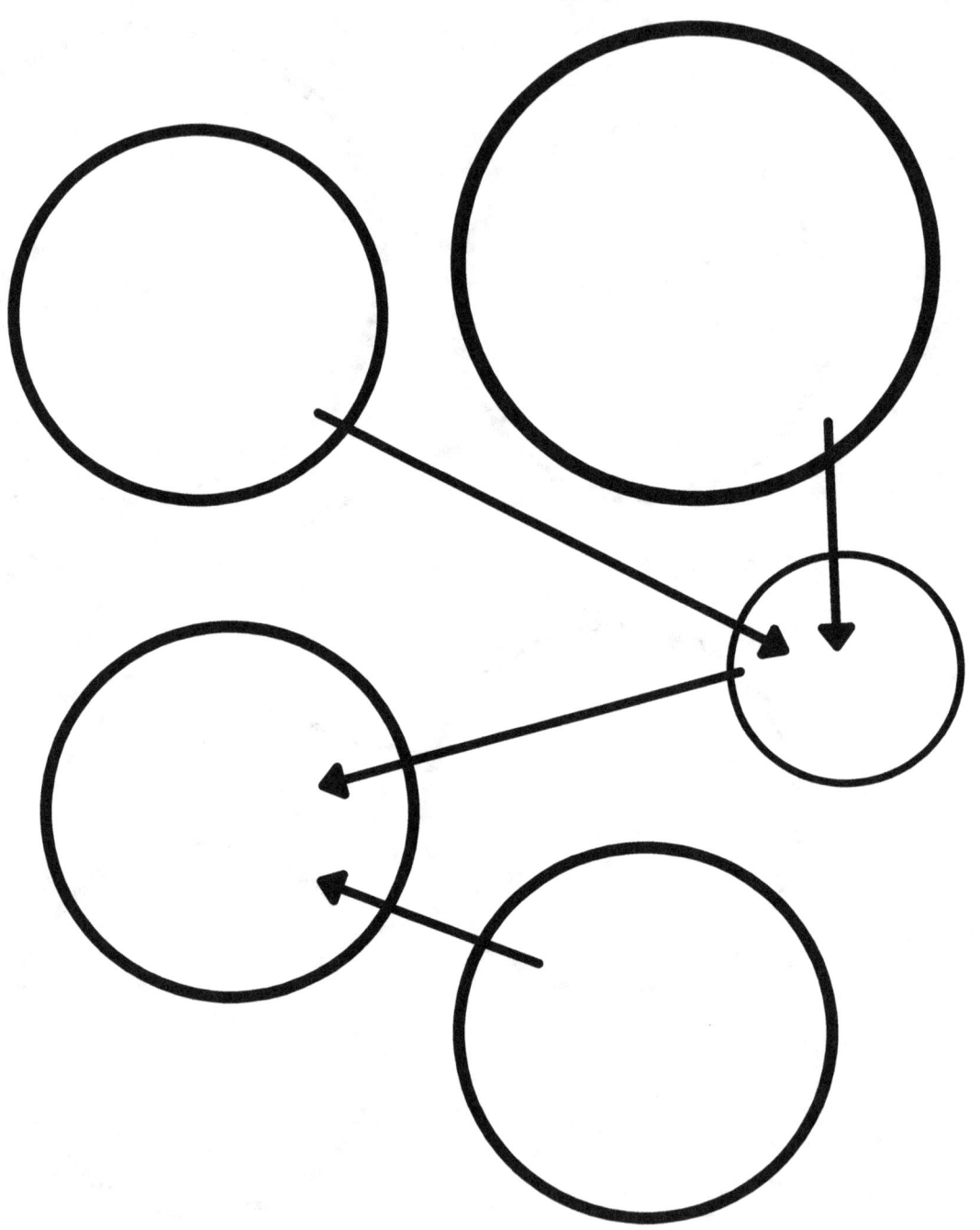

IDEAS

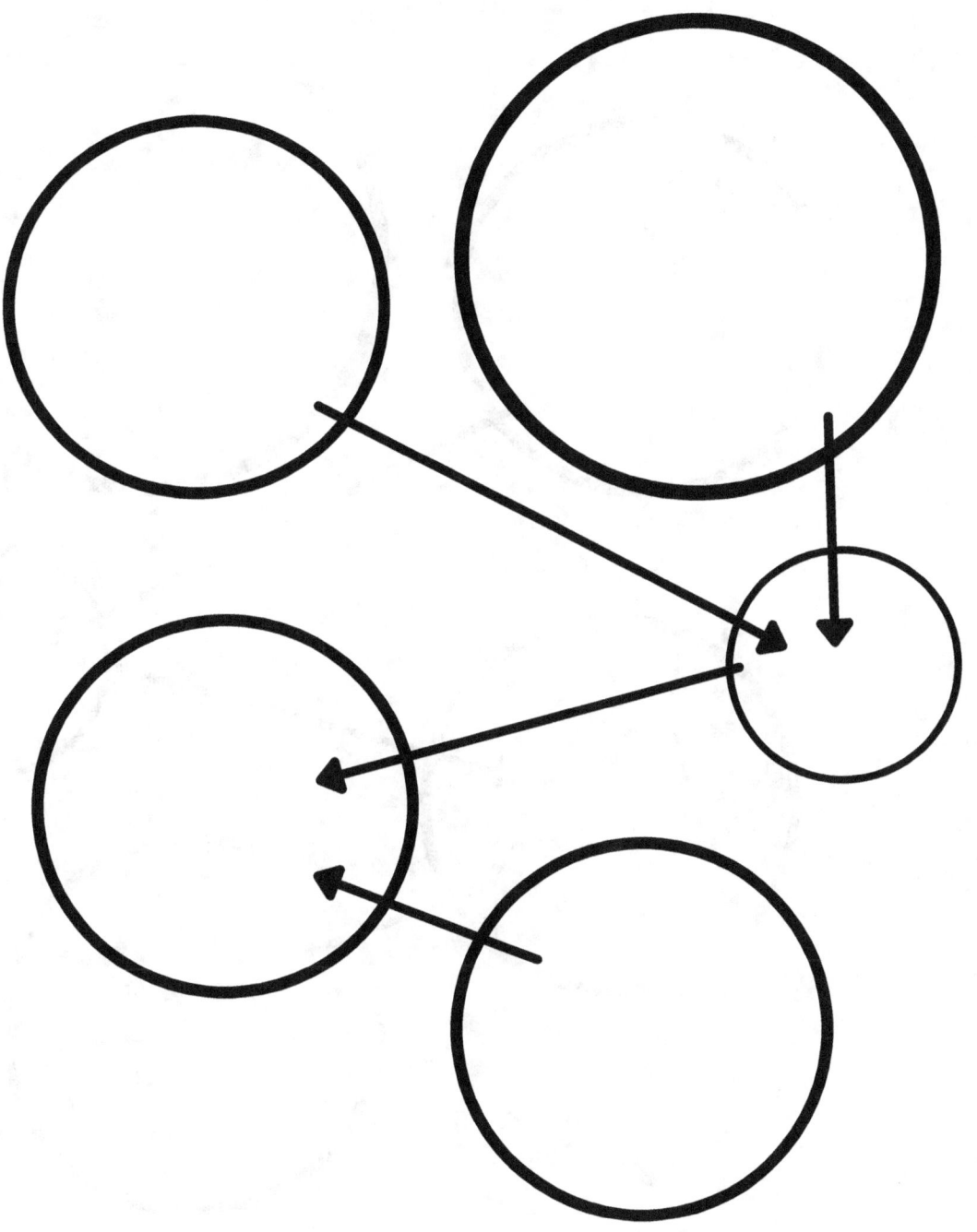

IDEAS

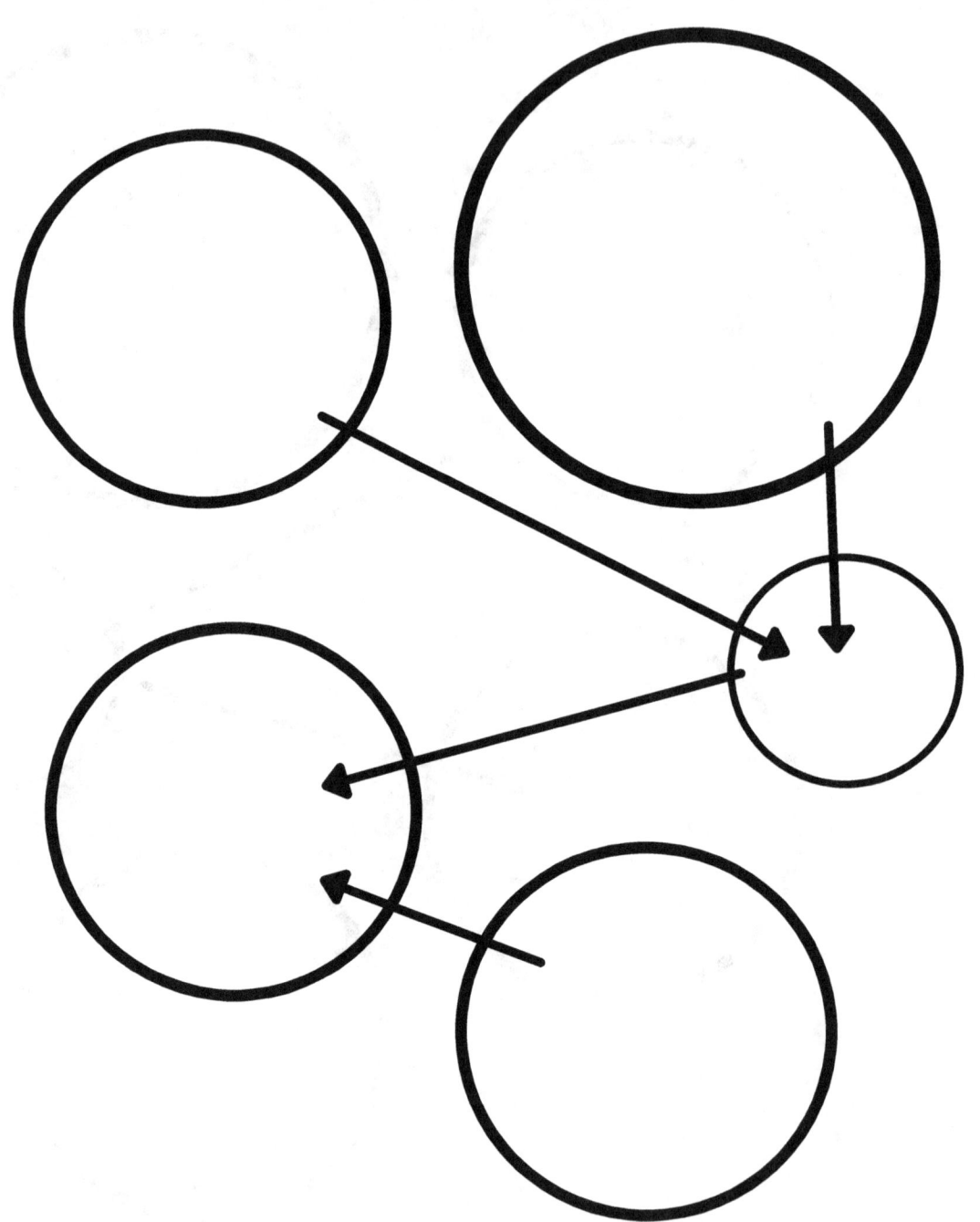

IDEAS

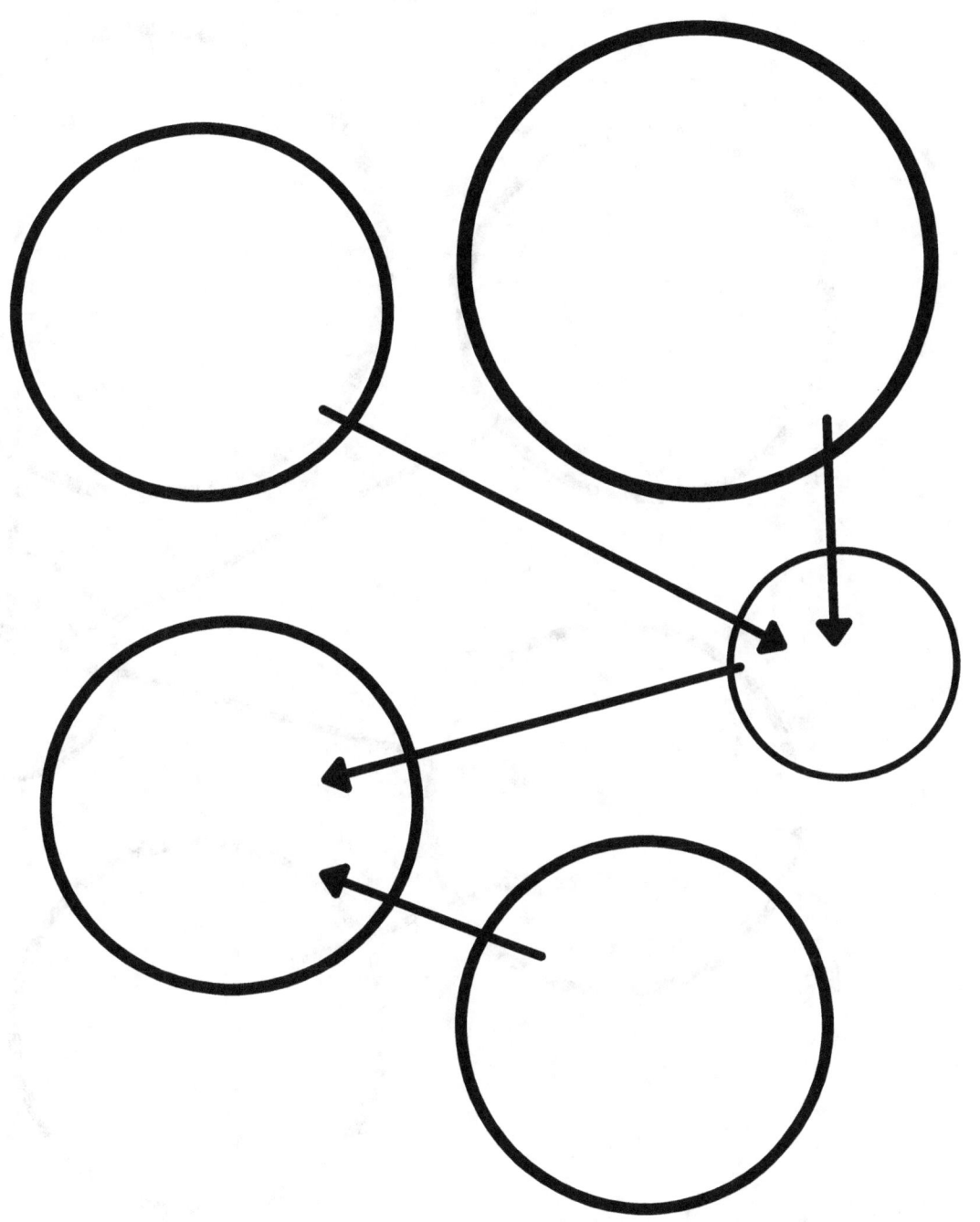

IDEAS

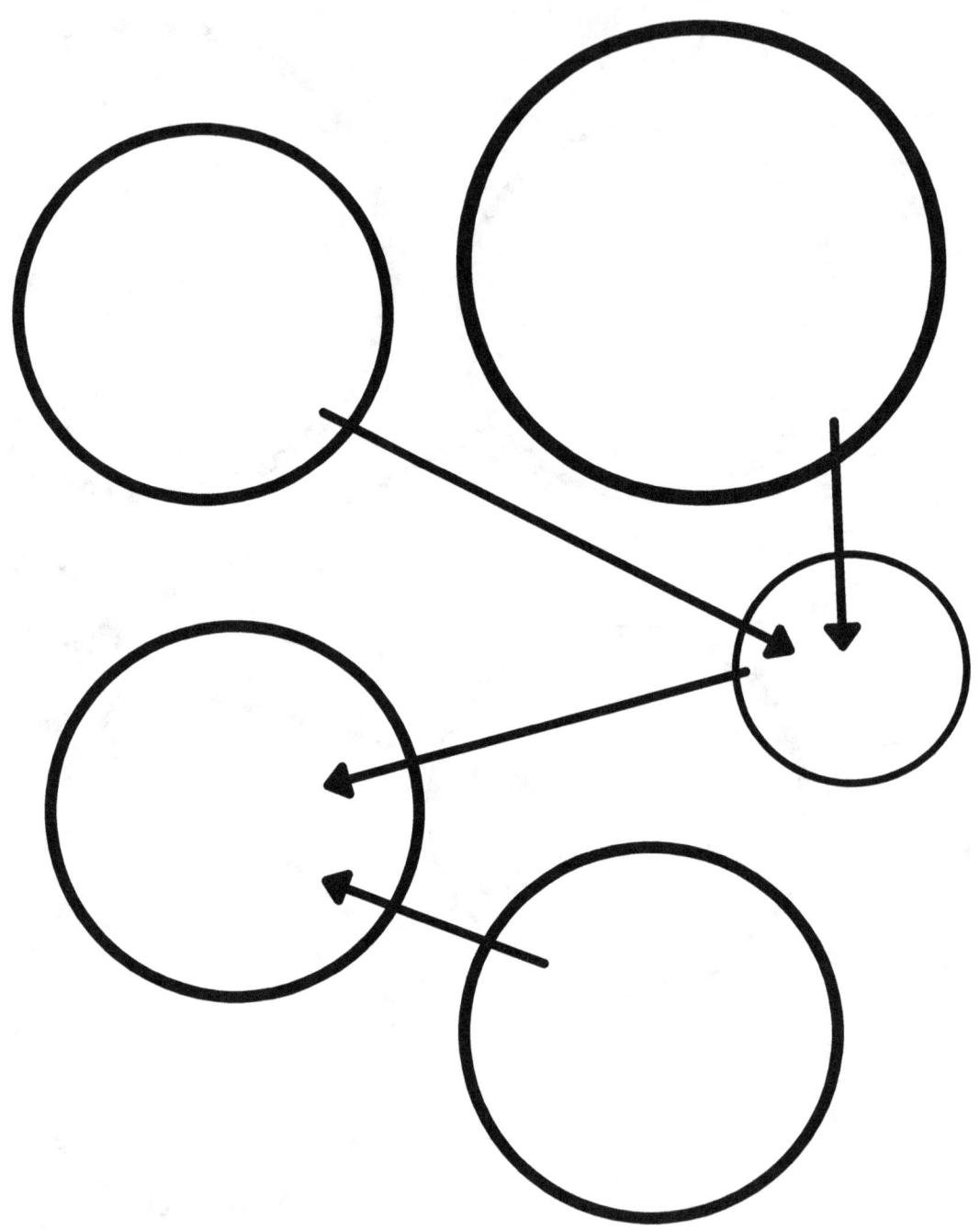

IDEAS

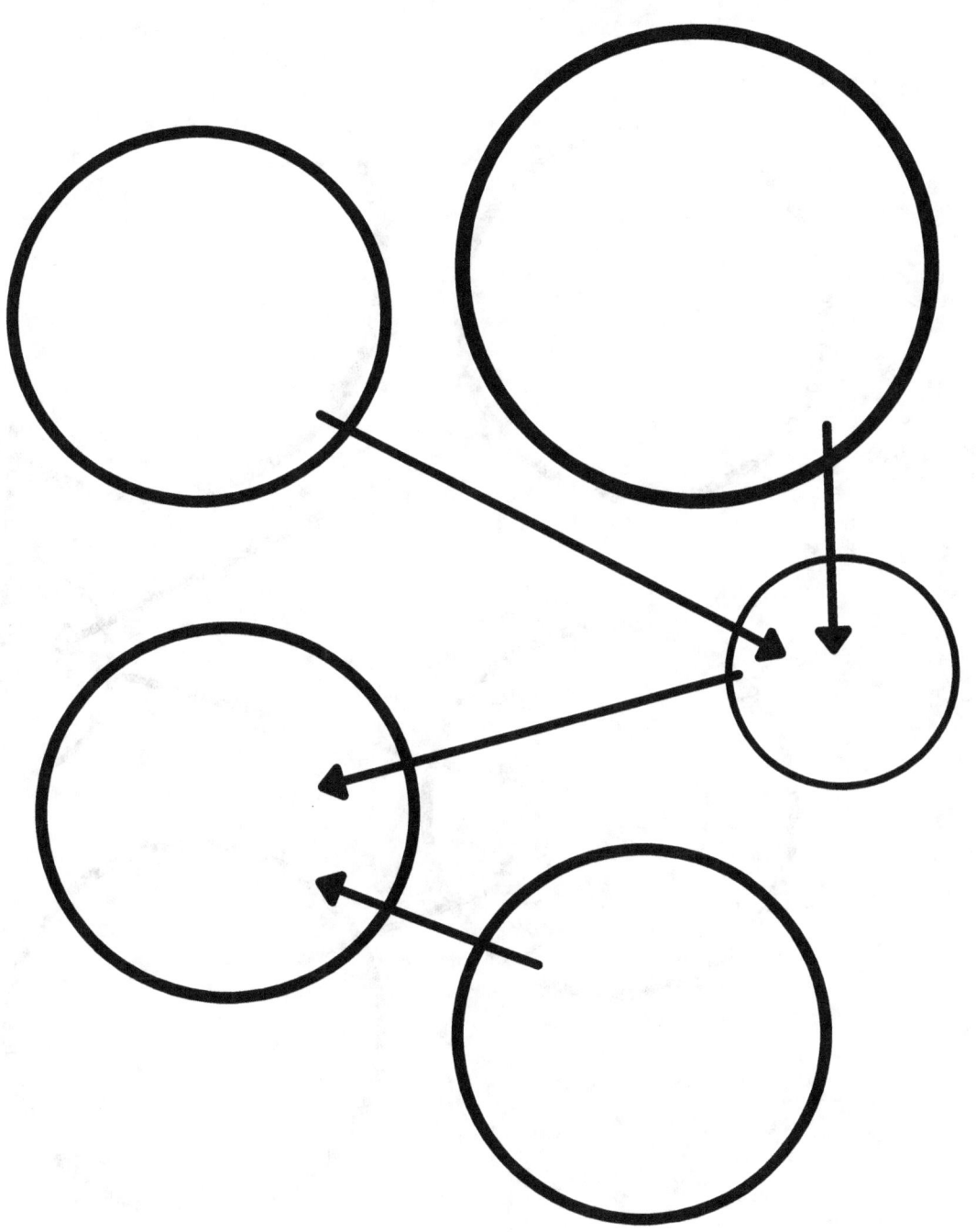

IDEAS

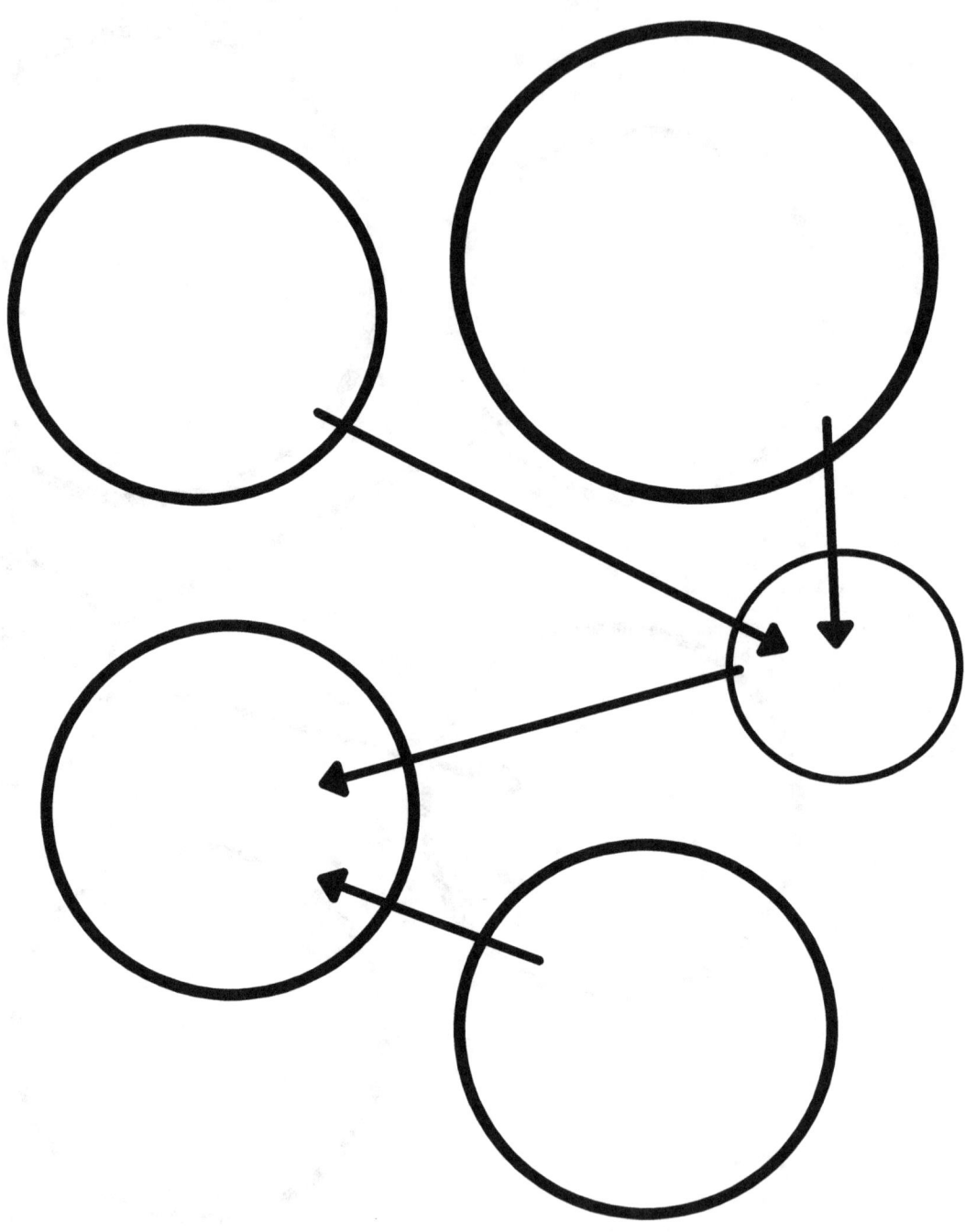

IDEAS

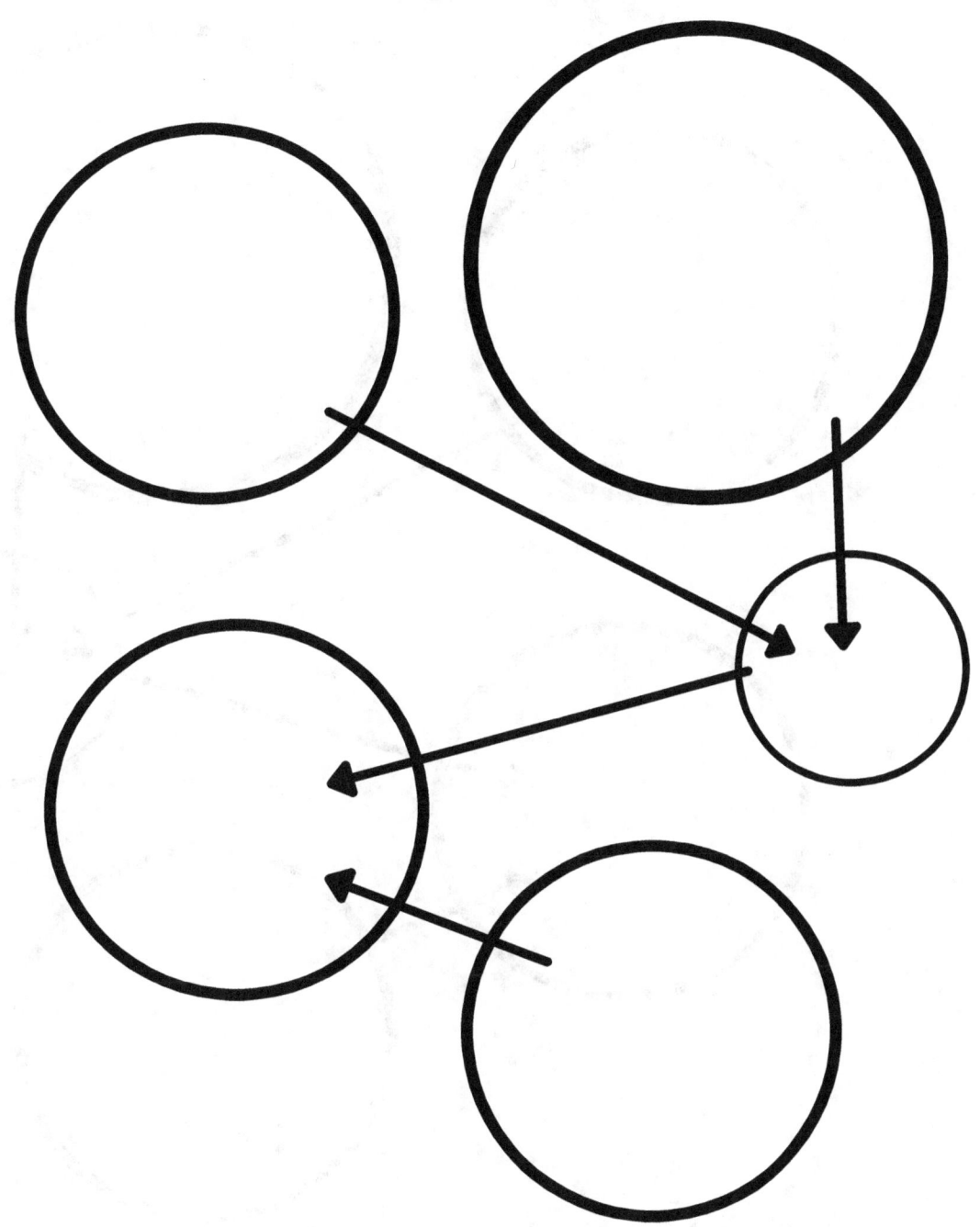

IDEAS

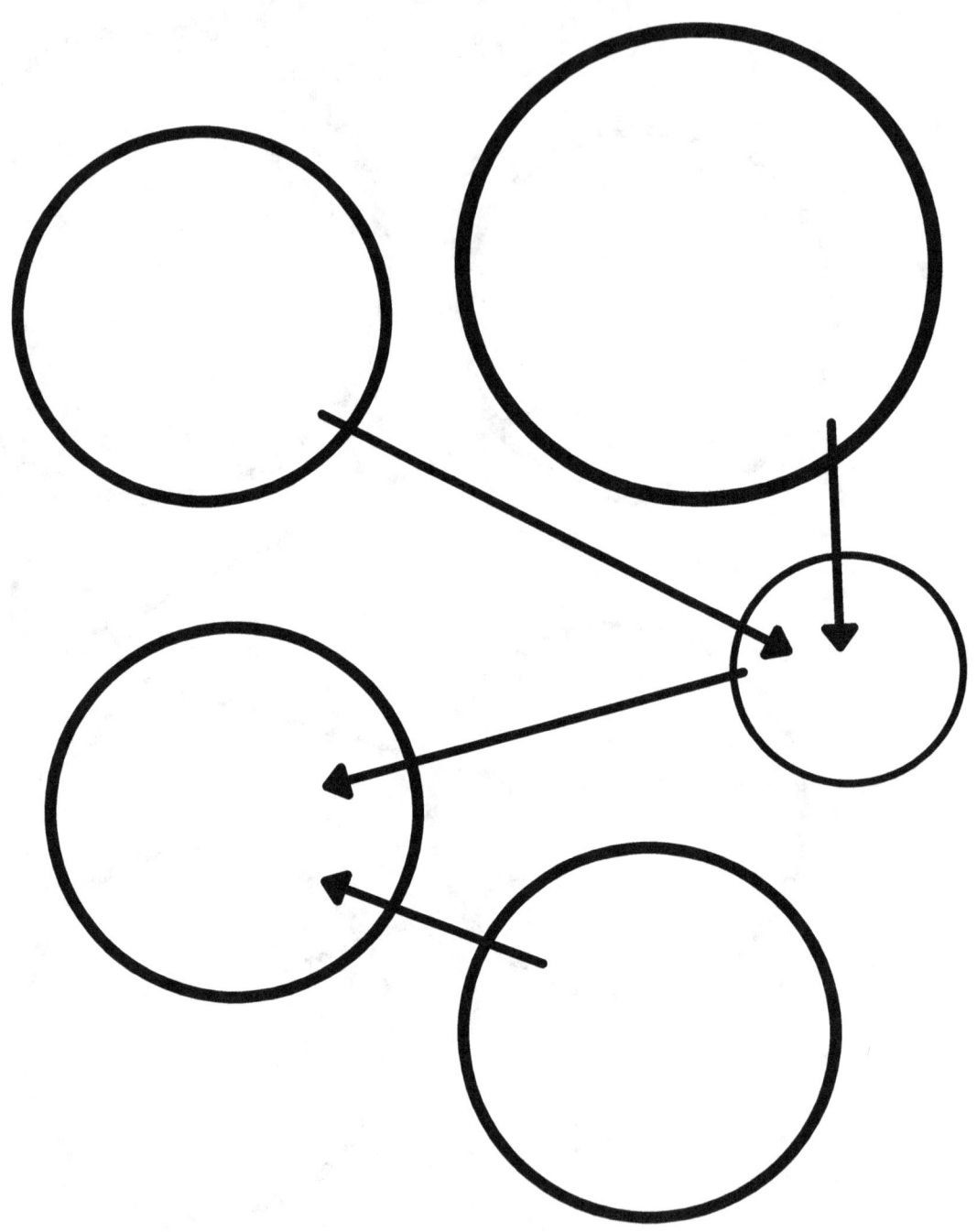

IDEAS

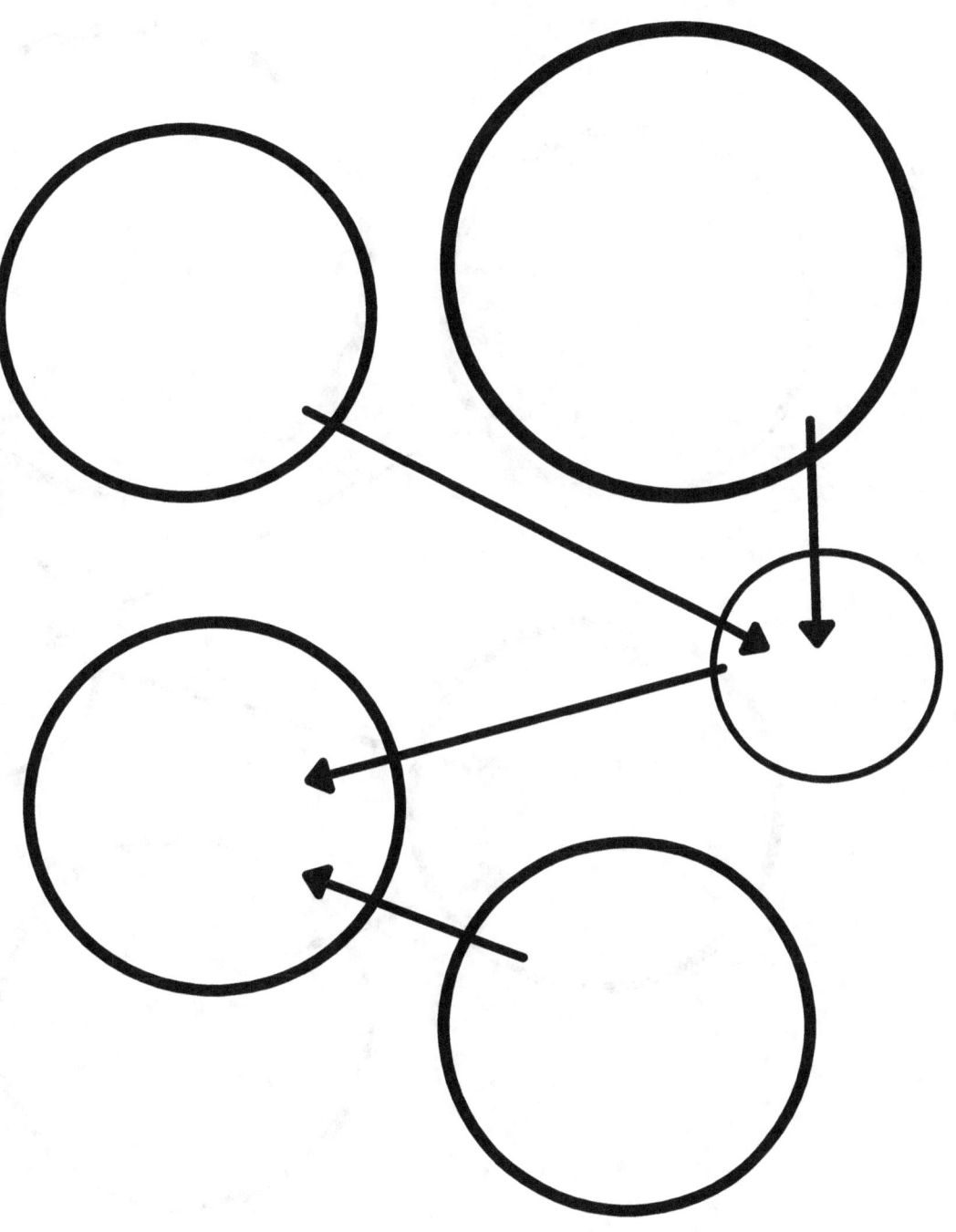

IDEAS

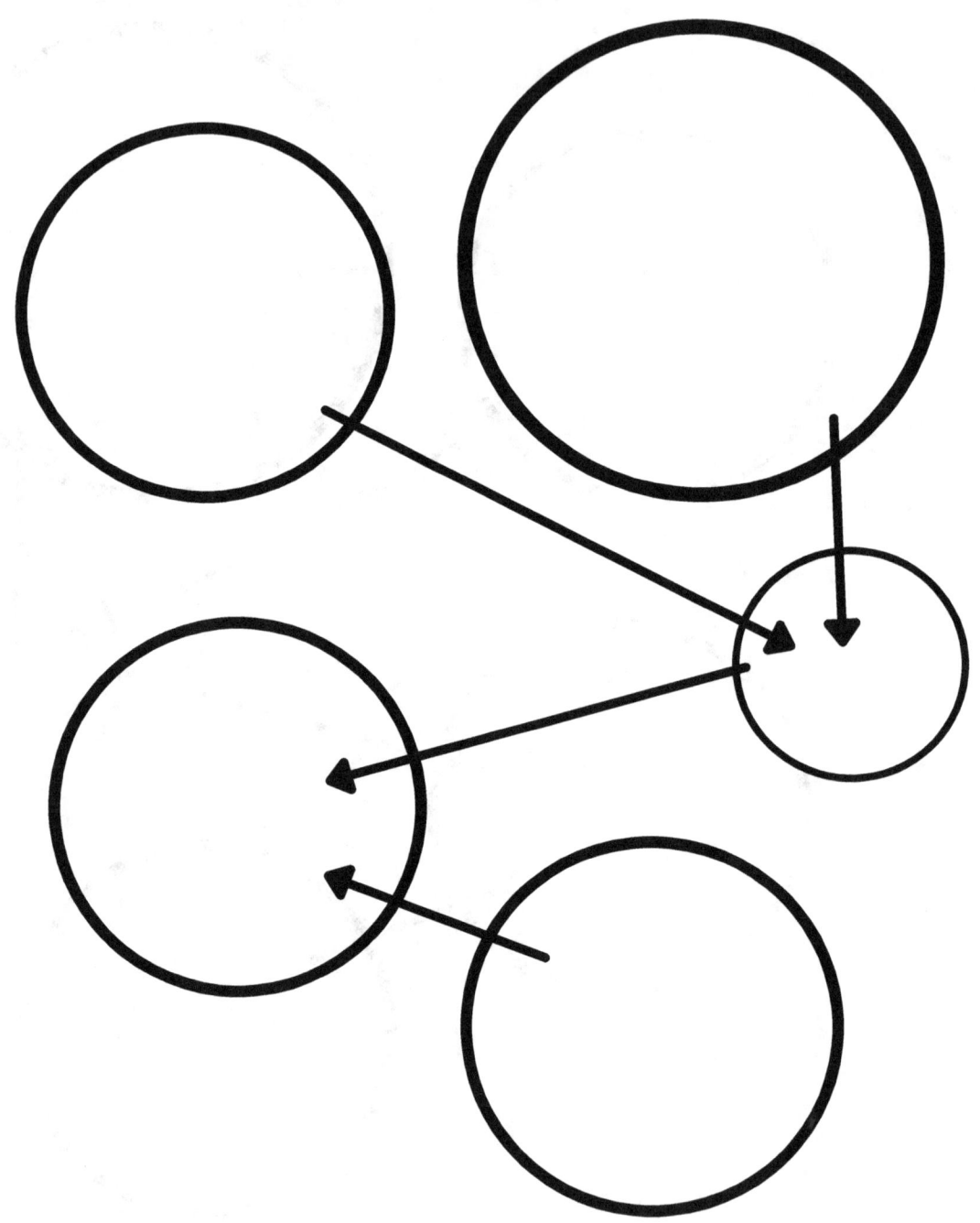

IDEAS

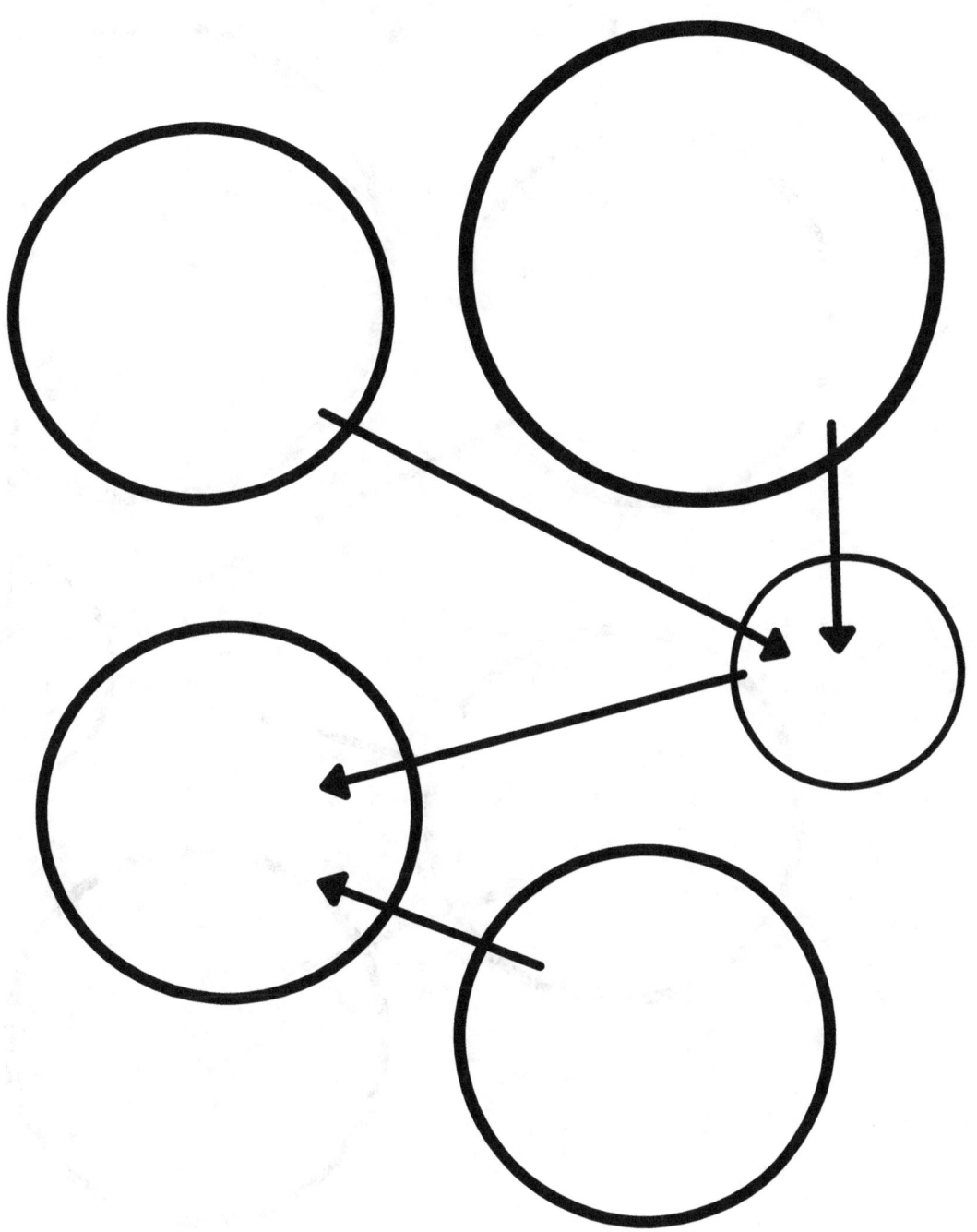

IDEAS

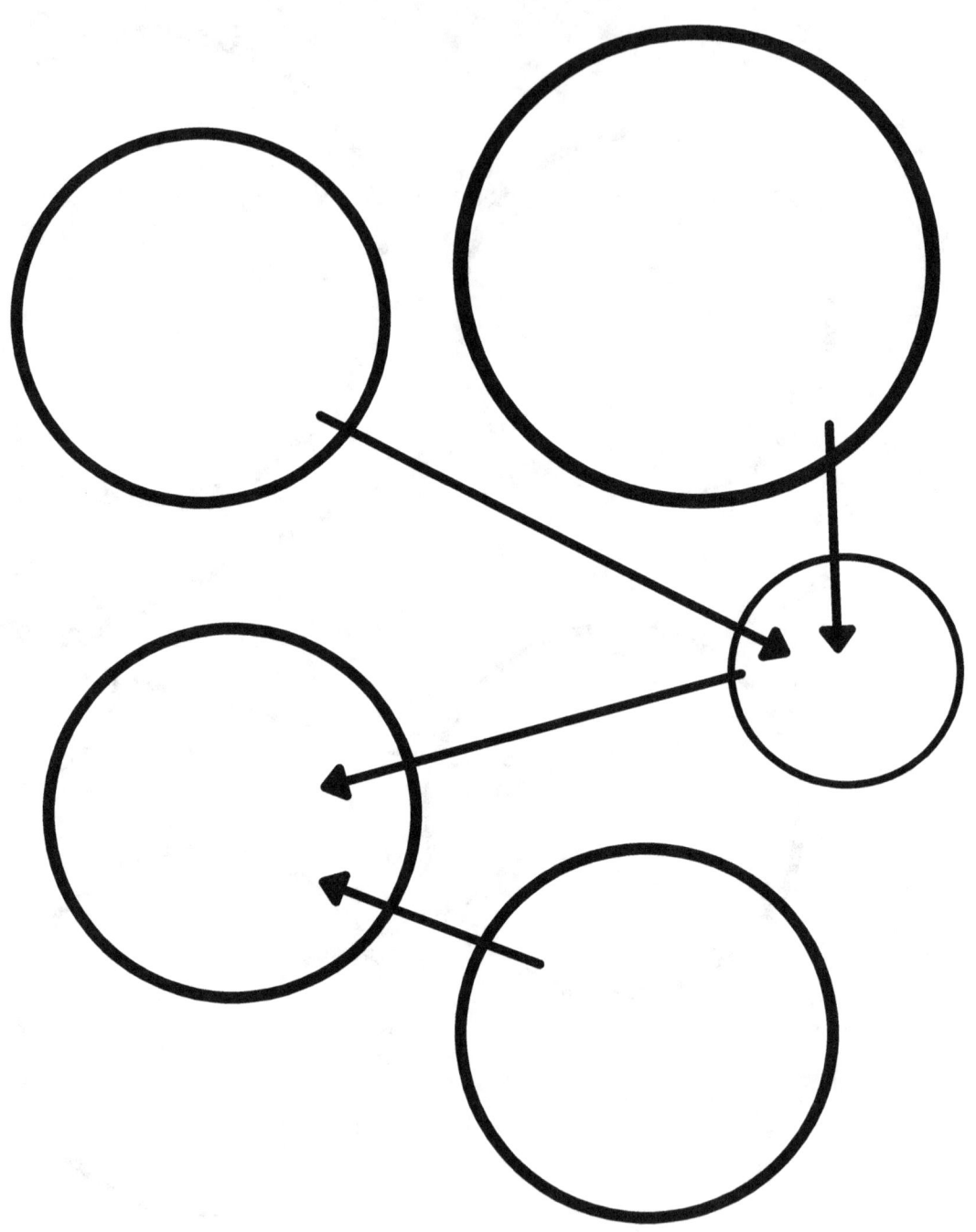

IDEAS

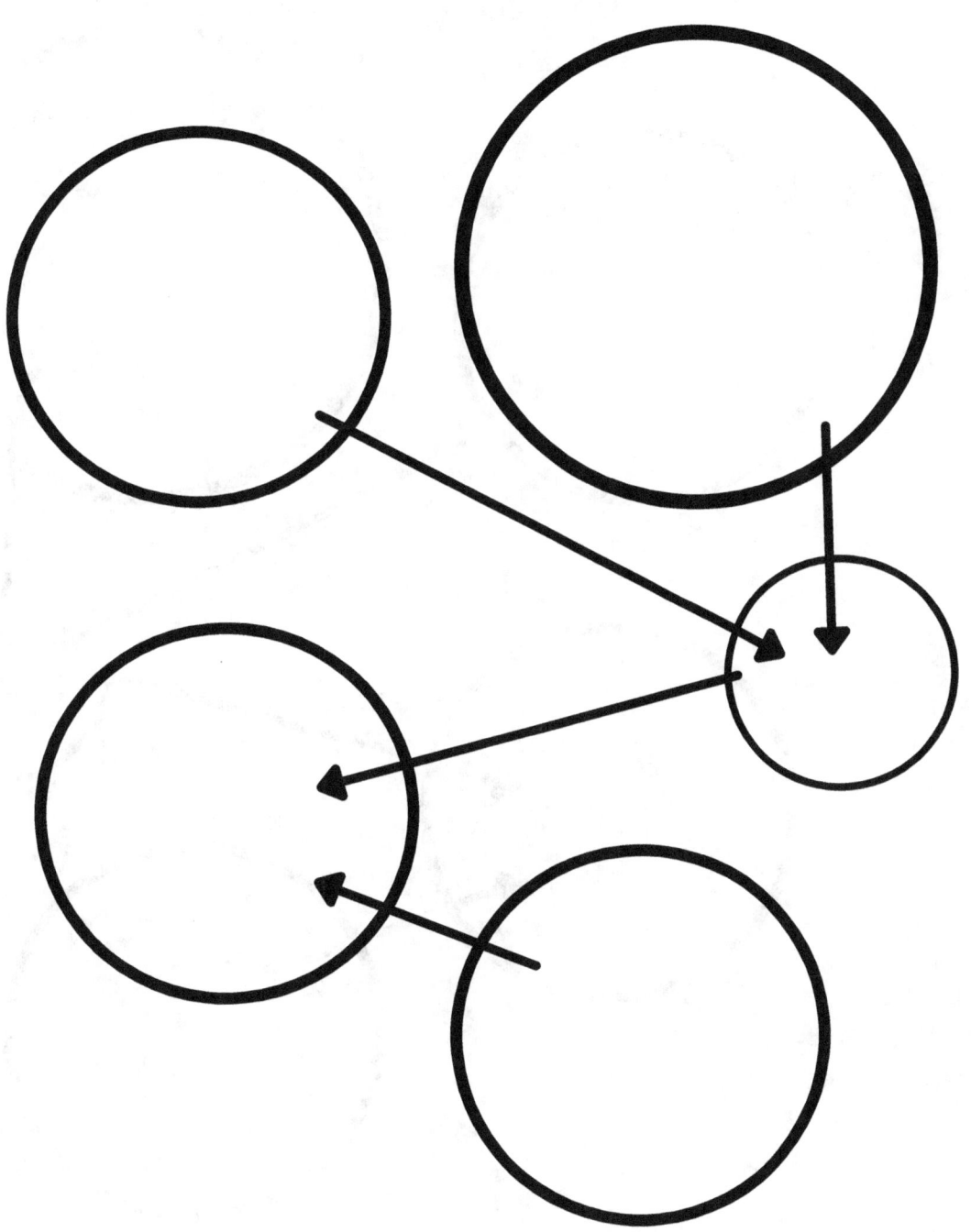

IDEAS

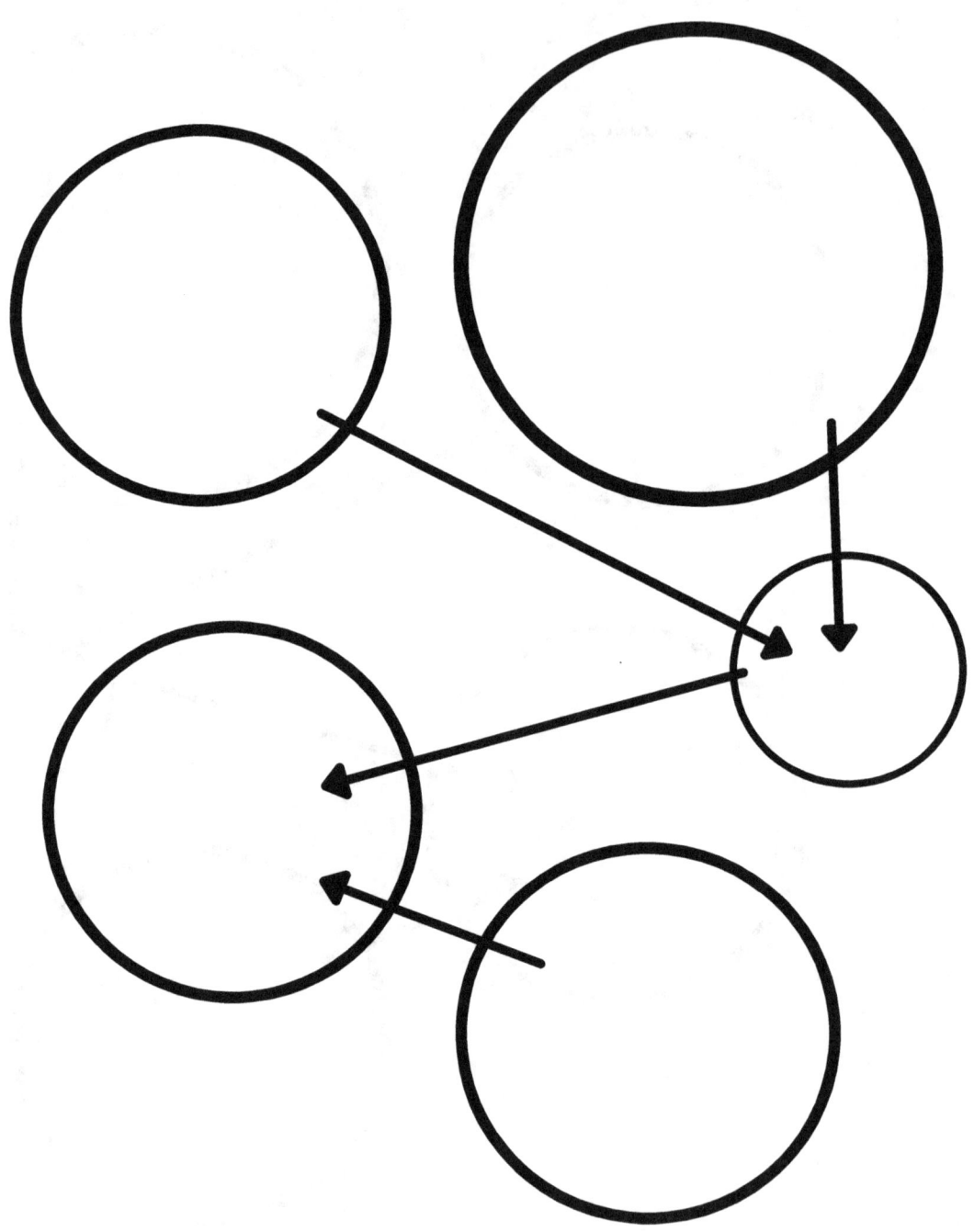

www.ingramcontent.com/pod-product-compliance
Lightning Source LLC
Chambersburg PA
CBHW081613220526
45468CB00010B/2865